The Expat Arc

An expat's journey over culture shock

danielle barkhouse

Danielle Barkhouse
www.daniellebarkhouse.com

Printed in the United States of America

ISBN-10 1434844730
EAN-13   9781434844736

First Edition, April 2008

To JB

Without you, Connor and I wouldn't have had
the opportunity to slide around on rainbows.

To Family

For supporting me through my toughest transition yet.

To Friends

Thank you for continuing to make room for me in your
address books, long after the "B" pages have been filled.

It's Official...We're Moving to India

Happy New Year! I hope everyone has started 2007 on the right foot! Unfortunately, I wasn't very organized this past Christmas and only managed to send out 50% of our Christmas greetings. If you didn't hear from us at Christmas, please forgive me! Here's what been happening...

After sitting on pins and needles since December, it's official; we're moving to India! We'll be living in Chennai which is on the east coast in southern India. We thought this might be a good time to start a web log. We'll be able to add photos along the way and keep our friends and family updated. We anticipate the announcement of JB's new job to be posted at work next week. After that we can get the ball rolling with visas, moving and selling our house. I met with our realtor this week about putting our house on the market. We're looking forward to (hopefully) selling it quickly.

We've been doing a lot of research online over the past few weeks. We don't have all the answers yet. Actually, we don't even have all our questions yet! So, watch this space! We'll keep writing as we know more.

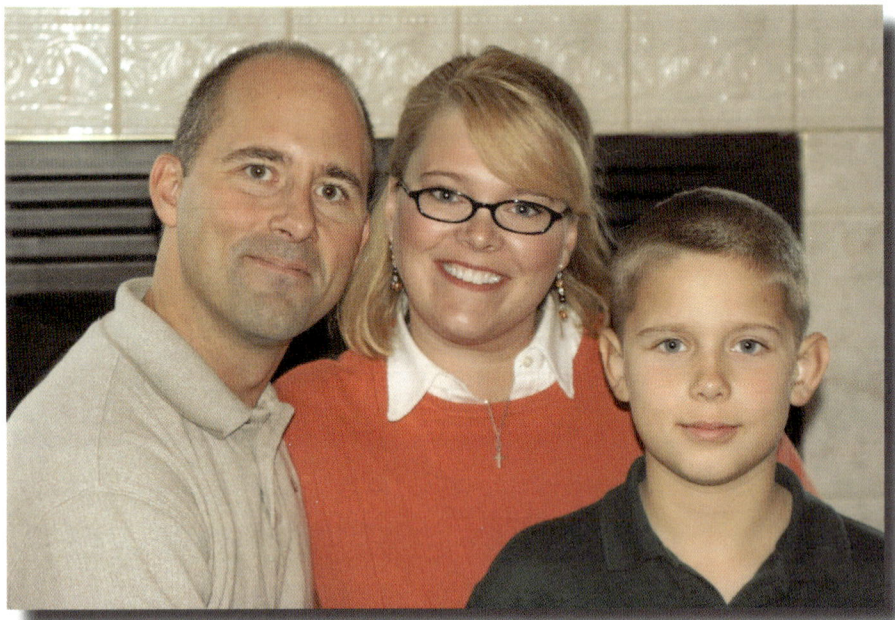

"You will also learn to make use of the quarterly shipment that the company provides."

Seriously, I made JB stop reading the email that he received from a co-worker in Chennai this morning and said, "Look at the goose bumps all over my legs!" So, now that it's official JB was able to look up other company folks in India and get some information. We received a very nice (and long) letter from someone in another department who lives in Bangalore. Here are few snippets from his letter:

"The housing in Chennai is good."

"There are 3 major things that you have to get used to; the poverty, the dirt, and driving around. The poverty is everywhere but usually will only effect expats to the point where we get hounded out in public by beggars. They are not dangerous though and will not bother your son. India is not very clean and that takes some getting used to, but again it will not effect you at work or home. Driving is always interesting and when I say driving I mean riding in the car, as you and your wife will both have personal drivers. Although there are not a lot of accidents, the driving is sporadic and very annoying, everyone uses their horns all the time, but you will get used to it. Also traffic can be a nightmare, especially at night, but again you just time it right and deal with it. The time it can take to go somewhere, even mid day is probably the most frustrating thing for my wife. So when you select a car for her, make sure it is comfortable."   I tend to agree...A comfortable car please!

"Medical care in India is very good. If your son or wife gets sick they can go to a doctor who will probably have practiced in the US. My son had strep a couple months back and so my wife (who is a pediatric RN) took him to the doctor and they gave him a prescription and that was it. There is also a very good hospital in Chennai. Hopefully you will never go there, but from what I hear it is excellent."

"Also for your wife. She will learn to be very patient here if she is not already, or she will get frustrated and not enjoy it. When she calls someone to come install the cable or fix something, they will promise her they will show up at 10am, but will not come until 4pm or not until the next day, and sometimes not at all. Also Indian culture favors men, so she will probably learn to get a bit aggressive to get what she wants. I don't say this in a bad way, but have had many experiences where my wife will ask someone to do something and they tell her, "Yes ma'am," and don't do it. I come home and ask for it and it gets done immediately. But, India is not like the Middle East where women can't go out in public alone or anything of that nature. Also make sure that you get a driver you can trust. The drivers will become a vital part of your life here in India and if you get good ones like we have, will help your wife out immensely." Y'all know I'm not the most patient person on earth. Leave it to God to provide the opportunity for me to grow :)

We were dancing around the kitchen this morning over this...

"Not sure if you have any pets? If so let me know and I will tell you how to get them in. We have 2 dogs and a Green winged Macaw (parrot). Dogs and Cats, no problem....the bird was an absolute nightmare. So hopefully you don't have a bird!!!!" Nope, no bird, but Kramer is very excited at the prospect of living in India!

I was also in touch with another American woman who's children go to the American International School of Chennai. She was a wealth of information as well. Here are a few snips from her email:

"Regarding the school: School here runs from early August (this year started August 9th) to early June. There's a 2 month summer break that doesn't coincide with the local summer break (March/April/May time). The city empties out of expats during the summer."

"Mosquitoes: Miserable. And they carry -everything-. Anything that can be carried by mosquitoes is in India. We've already had our 5yo go through Dengue, a month into our stay here. That was unpleasant. Malaria is a minor issue, but still present and thankfully not the fatal version we had to watch for in Togo. Chikungunya was practically epidemic for a while, but seems to have abated. I have 2 kids covered in various bites right now from mosquitoes to red ants, daily Off! or other repellent is an absolute must, in my opinion. Room repellents in the house are helpful too, and everyone has mosquito racquets, these electrified tennis racquet things you wave around, especially useful in the car since mosquitoes love to hang out in the cars at night."

"Poisonous spiders and snakes: As far as I know, not too many issues with poisonous spiders. Snakes, well, they're everywhere. We have a little snake sanctuary in our yard, something we can't quite get rid of for some reason, and a singular reason for having a gardener :) Since we've been here, only one snake has been reported to me and it was only about elbow length. Our neighbors a couple doors down had a 5' python in a tree in their yard a short while after arriving here, so.... You never know."

"Dress: Dress conservative, but that doesn't mean a full length skirt at all times. Just don't be obvious :) I wear my jeans and T-shirts out and about, but I don't wear sleeveless shirts or shorts. I don't wear anything that shows any leg, actually. Around here, the local dress for women is the saree or the salwar kameez so as long as I'm covered about the same, I feel I'm doing my part."

I have to admit the mosquitoes freak me out. I'll be counting on a quarterly shipment of Deep Woods OFF! This will give you a better idea of what life will be like for us in India.

In other news, we have not located Connor's Canadian citizenship card. For people with dual citizenship, there is a risk that a consulate won't help them if they enter a country on a passport of their other citizenship, ie: Canada Consulate wouldn't help Connor if he entered on a US passport. The card is needed to get his Canadian passport. That whole process would take 6-8 months to complete and we would likely have to stay behind until it's done. JB has contacted the legal dept. at work to see if Connor can enter on his US passport and have a new visa in 8 months time when his Canadian paperwork is complete. We'll know more about that soon.

What Pets Do to a Family

Our oldest cat, Sylvester, is 16 years old. He's lived in three countries and four states. He's in good health, but he's old. He's endured several long flights in his lifetime and was quarantined for 6 months when we lived in England. Sylvester has been a house guest with family members and friends over the years as we've been in varying states of transition. Since he has a "Garfield" attitude, he goes with the flow.

Then there's Francesca...Frannie-Girl. She's 11 years old, tiny, very timid and she loves me. Frannie will curl herself around until she's upside down for her armpits and ears to rubbed. When I was pregnant with Connor, she napped with me and paid me a ton of attention. It's hard not to love her, if you get the chance to meet her (when she's not hiding) you just can't help but love her, everyone does.

And Kramer; he's our golden retriever who is 2 and a half years old. He's bad-mannered, ill-tempered and very possessive of me. He doesn't like anyone in the family hugging me and shows his annoyance when strangers are around me. But I just love that stinkin' mutt. When JB's away, he sleeps with me. When JB is home, he sleeps next my bed. And now, I just can't sleep without him. He only minds me and thinks everyone else is a joker. Connor loves Kramer. Every boy should have a dog to play with.

We love our pets so much and they love us. They add something indescribable to our family. Initially, we left our pets behind with friends when we moved to the UK because we didn't want them to go through quarantine. We were so fortunate to have friends willing to do that for us, but when we got there it was too hard without them. I would look down at my feet before backing up or taking a step in the kitchen because they were usually there, but then they weren't. I trudged back to the US to get them so I could fill that gaping hole in my heart.

And now India; the flight is just too long and the temperatures too varying to put Sylvester and Fran through it again. This morning while Fran was curled up on me for her tummy rub, it all hit me and I started to cry. Today is a "boo" day. I hate the thought of leaving our cat, for good this time. After enjoying all the US has to offer, I feel that just relocating our family--while, yes, it will be an adventure--in some ways is sacrifice enough. We're giving up enough and I don't want to give up our cats too. Kramer is coming with us. He's young enough and healthy enough. He stands a better chance of doing OK on the long flight. Kramer was Connor's reward when we came back to the US, there's no way I can take an only child's best friend away from him. Taking Kramer with us is creating big complications to set a moving date and arranging temporary housing. We'll see how that works out but I'm not leaving without him.

I'm grateful that Fran is going to my friend in NC, who I know loves her as much as I do. I know that the children will love her and she'll be well taken care of. We're still making arrangements for Sylvester, but if his current adopting family (my sister) comes through, I won't worry about him there either. They'll both be in good hands and they'll both be loved...it just won't be me there to love them.

Pets add so much to a family. They create large voids when they're gone, though. People who don't have pets or don't like animals don't understand this. For those of us that do, it takes a long time for the hurt and the grief to ease.

Ode to the Expats

The definition of expatriate is 'living in a foreign land. So, technically, I'm an expat living in the US. That never actually occurred to me until now and it sounds kind of comical to be a Canadian expat living in the US. Who cares, right?

I don't know why, but I've never read a book about being an expat or about repatriation. This time, I'm tapping into every available resource. I've done the research and I'm educating myself about the country we'll call home for the next three years. I'm researching and educating myself about life as an expat, parenting abroad and what it will all mean after we repatriate.

An expat friend sent me a link and I've been surfing the internet into the night. So, this one is for all my expat friends:

www.expatwomen.com - A new website but I think it will be fabulous when people begin to participate.

www.expatexpert.com - I've just ordered several of Robin Pascoe's books. I'm looking forward to reading *Raising Global Nomads* and *A Moveable Marriage*. She has a blog and chat forum link on her website.

http://www.livingabroadmagazine.com/ - A UK-based magazine for expats

www.GlobeSmart.com - This is the company/website that provided our cultural training. I'm not certain if the website is accessible only through a corporate employer but if you can get to it, it's a wealth of information.

I was quite fortunate that when we returned to the US, we were assigned to a new location. Essentially, repatriating was just another expat location for me. I met some American expats during our time in the UK and they had a much harder time readjusting when they came back here to their hometown. Perhaps this is why I feel like a fish out of water when I go back to my hometown in Canada?

Here are two books that I found tonight. A little light reading material while I'm hanging by the pool, perhaps?

Homeward Bound: A Guide to Repatriation by Robin Pascoe

The Art of Coming Home by Craig Storti

I also ordered a book or two about expat careers and expat entrepreneurs. If there is one thing I learned in 2006, it was that if I ever want to have a career of my own, it would have to be one that worked well around JB's career. Essentially, it would have to be a career that I could pack in a suitcase. The good news is, it's only taken me 15 years to figure that one out and to stop going against the grain. I'm a quick learner!

So, yesterday, I was crying about my cat. Tonight, in the middle of the night, I'm excited about our next expat adventure. Welcome to my white knuckle emotional roller coaster...around here, we just call that being an "Expat."

🚩 60% Cheaper Than Concrete

Let me start off by saying that a house in India with decent water and power (and not too long of a commute for JB) was enough for me, but a pool was a big bonus. In fact, it was a bonus that JB made an effort for us to have. Unfortunately, the house he found didn't have one. We were so pleased when the landlord agreed to put one in. Press button, "That was easy!"

When JB returned from our house-hunting trip in Chennai, we emailed back and forth with our agent so that our requests (and the landlord's intentions) would be written in the lease. The landlord suggested a fiberglass pool instead of concrete one because it would take less time to install and would be 60% cheaper. We said, "OK". We had just researched pools last spring when we considered putting one in our own backyard so we had a pretty good visual of what he meant. Or did we?

We received a pool brochure yesterday for our approval. I asked JB if he specified in-ground or above ground. He emailed the agent back to reiterate that we would prefer an in-ground pool. She responds with, "Oh yes, here is the pool, it will be 6" above ground.

On the brochure it says "Above Ground." If they were in-ground, I'm thinking the brochure would say, "In Ground Pools." Or, "Above Ground Pools With An In Ground Option." Or, "Go Ahead, Bury The Above Ground Pool."

🚩 Regret and Relief

I had a light bulb moment this morning. I've been alternating reading *Survival Kit for Overseas Living* by L. Robert Kohls and *Homeward Bound* by Robin Pascoe. One book is about leaving home to live abroad and the other is about coping with your return home.

My regret is that I didn't make our assignment in England all that it could be. I spent three years doing what I could just to get by. It never felt like home, but I never let it. From the time that I arrived, I felt as though my life was going on in North Carolina only I wasn't there to live it. I knew we were in England for three years and I started counting down the time as soon as I arrived. Part of it may have been my age, that we homeschooled, that we moved there two days before 9/11, or that I just wasn't prepared for the expat experience. We met wonderful people, traveled, and had tremendous experiences or moments, but on the whole I can see that I wasted three years. What a shame.

My newfound relief is that when I came back to the US, everything that I went through mentally and emotionally was normal. I had an identity crisis and I wasn't sure how to go about making new friends. Perhaps it wouldn't have been so traumatic if I had known what to expect. How about that? I'm (somewhat) normal after all. What a relief.

The light bulb is on and I can see things a little more clearly.

🚩 Passport Pains

I've spent the last two weeks trying to reach Passport Canada by phone. When I finally get to a call queue, there's a recording that says they've reached the maximum allowable people on hold, then I get disconnected. Two weeks ago, the charge went through my bank account for my passport. I'm still waiting for it. I applied for it back in January. I couldn't reach them by phone so I sent an email inquiry. They said to allow five days for a response, it took thirteen days. I'm surprised I received an answer at all. The email stated that my passport would be shipped the week of March 12. That means I won't have enough time to get my visa (it takes two weeks) before our March 23 target date. The email also said that if I needed my passport more urgently to call the toll free number provided. Yeah, that's the same number I've been calling for two weeks without getting through.

Today was my turn, I had a colossal meltdown. I guess I was due.

Checking off the checklist...

Full day of cultural training: check.

Providing writing samples, voice samples, fingerprints, photos of identifying jewelry, and dental records in the event of a natural disaster, accident or criminal act: check.

Physicals, dentist appointments, immunizations: check, check, check.

Filling massive prescriptions for allergy and malaria medications: check, check.

Find a house in India: check.

Apply to school in India: in progress.

Arrange pet shipping for Kramer: in progress.

Book a hotel room for a month long stay in Illinois: check.

Find temporary housing in India that allows a dog for an additional month long stay: check.

Have dinner at Sizzling India every other week to open Connor to Indian food: check.

Place stickers on everything we own labelled Storage, Air Freight, Sea Freight: in progress.

Finish up our shopping: in progress.

Address moving announcements: check.

Forwarding mail: in progress.

Arranging an Illinois phone number for our friends and family to reach us in India: check.

Disconnect utilities: check.

Ready for the packers to arrive on Monday morning at 7:30am: noooooo comment.

Denial and Avoidance

Everyone copes in different ways. Today, I'm choosing the denial and avoidance method.

I've given the movers my cell phone number, rescheduled my doctor appointment and came back to the hotel.

I changed back into my jammies, crawled back into bed with my dog and had a wonderful nap.

Since I'm denying and avoiding so well today, a sleeve of Girl Scout Thin Mints for lunch couldn't hurt either, right?

And the showing of our house that has been scheduled for today--day three of packing--yep, denying and avoiding that too.

I'm going to stay in this happy world until 3:30pm today. Until then, Do Not Disturb. I'm disturbed enough all on my own.

Then and Now

Flashback to North Carolina, September 7, 2001:

Our first small house that we built was empty. The movers were gone and I just couldn't bring myself to go back inside. I didn't (couldn't) do the move-out cleaning. I just knew going into that abandoned house would open a flood that would probably still be flowing today. I cried and cried and cried when we drove away from Yates Garden Lane. Talk about drama.

Illinois, March 2, 2007:

Our house is empty but for a few flammable items that couldn't be shipped. There are also bits of paper everywhere left behind by the packers and plenty o' dust. I've decided to hire someone to do the move-out clean. Other than our house in NC (JB did the clean by himself), I've always done it.

After school we stopped by the house to see how the loading was going, but the movers were done and gone. We went inside. The rooms were completely empty and there was an echo in the house. I'm not sure why, but I didn't feel sad. Maybe the sadness will come later, I'm not sure. Walking around, I felt relief.

I have to admit that when we moved into that house, I thought it would be the last house we would ever own. I thought that even if we did another foreign assignment we would keep the house forever. Slowly that changed over the three and a half years of living there, along with the multiple disputes our sue-happy-retired-and-have-nothing-better-to-do neighbors had with us.

Connor's bedroom was in the bonus-room above the garage. He had a really cool sports-themed room. He also has a really cool dad who built him a bed into the sloped ceilings, complete with bookshelves and lighting. Connor got midway into the room, fell on the floor and cried his heart out. While I was reminding him of the very cool locker furniture that would be waiting for him in India, my heart ached for him. Then I just sat quietly with him while he cried. This was his North Carolina. The bed that he and his dad built together, and he would never sleep in it again.

Connor cried again while hugging Kramer as I drove away. He perked up later when we met friends, neighbors and colleagues at an Irish pub for farewell drinks. Even some of Connor's friends were there too! We had a very nice evening. When we crawled into bed last night, JB said, "We have nice friends." Indeed we do.

Weekend Facts

- I asked the hotel to service our room while the dog was out of the hotel for grooming.

- I left the hotel at 11:45am to meet friends for lunch.

- After picking the dog up at the puppy spa, I arrived back at my hotel room around 1:45pm.

- When I arrived at my door, it was open. I called into the room to see if someone was there; no answer.

- Immediately, I called down to the front desk to tell them that when my room was cleaned the door had been left opened.

- The front desk staff informed me that the person who cleaned my room had left for the day. She asked me if anything had been taken. "No, my laptop and iPod are still on the table," I told her.

-Connor got home from school and couldn't find his brand new Nintendo DS Light.

- JB got home from university and wondered why his headphones were on the table but his brand new video iPod was not.

- I spent Saturday morning unpacking suitcases while checking pockets and backpacks for missing items...without success.

- When JB got home from class on Saturday, we went to front desk to tell them that there were items missing from our room.

- "The manager is on vacation until Monday," we were told.

- We came back to the room and JB took one last rifle through his computer bag. Wait, where's his company computer? Yes, the one with plenty of confidential company information and his Masters Thesis.

- We went downtown to file a police report for a stolen laptop computer and pc cellular card, a video iPod, and a Nintendo DS with Mario Cart game. We also reported the stolen property to the company.

- I don't want to stay in this hotel. I don't want to pack everything up (again) and move (again). We informed the staff that unless the building was on fire, nobody had permission to enter our room without me being here.

- And we were concerned about theft in India?

Priceless!

Moving and storage company to ship the overflow shipment of our household goods in a 20' sea container since they were too incompetent to provide an accurate estimate of volume: $7693.96

Air Animal for shipping Kramer exactly half-way around the world (cargo, not first-class): $6000

Pottery Barn Teen for non-built-in children's bedroom furniture: $3600

The thief who jacked our hotel room of a laptop, iPod and Nintendo DS: $3000

Land's End for summer clothes for the whole family: $2000

Sam's Club for pain relievers, fever-reducers, children's you-name-it meds, anti-bacterial and anti-diarrheal products, Ziploc bags and a few snacks (strange looks from other customers were free): $ 780

Target for two carts full of toiletries, minor first-aid supplies, underwear, bug spray, after-bite, sunscreen, hair color and Tassimo coffee cartridges: $780

CVS pharmacy for a 6 month supply of allergy meds and an unspecified amount of malaria meds: $390

Cub Foods for non-perishable favorite foods: $300

QVC for a year's worth of makeup and skin care products: $ 290

Petsmart for dog food: $192

Amazon.com for books about India, expat life and repatriation: $ 180

Old Navy for flip-flops and t-shirts: $ 153

Rain gear for two adults, one child and one dog: $ 115

Vistaprint for moving announcements and new address labels: $ 107

Joyce Meyer Ministries for Battlefield of the Mind Bible Study (medicine for the the 6 month stinkin' thinkin' phase but at this rate I might need it sooner): $ 80

Amazon.com (again) for more books; this time ranging from trashy to mildly intelligent for our flight: $ 58

FedEx for overnighting my passport to Atlanta twice since I didn't sign it before sending it to our immigration attorney the first time: $44

The experience of living in India for three years: Priceless!

Reverse Culture Shock

We went to Target yesterday to pick up all the things needed when living in a hotel...like, replacing the deodorant that my dog ate.

I quickly grabbed a very small bottle of dish soap and off I went to the next thing on my list. I came around the corner again and noticed an older Indian woman standing in front of the dish soap aisle. She looked so confused and so overwhelmed. I made myself busy but watched her to see what brand would catch her eye. She just stood there for a long time. Finally, she walked away empty handed.

I've had that same feeling before. In fact, I remember when I was trying to pick out laundry detergent in England. None of the brands were familiar. I developed a technique that if I stood there long enough, someone would come along and pick a brand. That's the one I would pick too. It took me a very long time to pick up a few basic groceries.

I know I'm going to go live in a place where choice of brand and/ or product is limited. I can't imagine what it was like for the Indian lady at Target. Not just to pick out dish soap but for daily life here in the US, land of plenty (and then some). I never really thought about reverse culture-shock.

It must really be shocking for people from other countries arriving in the US.

More Than a Feeling

Have you ever just had one of those feelings? The kind that make you stop where you are? You panic but you're not sure what action to take?

While it galls me every time I pull into this hotel parking lot, I didn't have a choice. We couldn't find another suite that would take a dog. It made me very angry when I would think about how I'm paying to stay at a hotel where I've been robbed. A hotel where their insurance company won't return any of my three calls to them. And I'm paying them daily for it.

Yesterday, I notified the hotel management that I would be in my room from 9:30am to 11:30am (with my dog) and that is when I would like to have my room serviced. While the housekeeper was servicing my room, a big guy came to the door and looked around my room while he was chatting up the housekeeper. At first, he didn't notice me sitting in the chair in the corner. I asked the housekeeper who the man is and she said, "He's from the maintenance department." She says he goes around to the rooms to make sure they're empty before housekeeping goes in. Got that feeling yet?

When I returned to the hotel later in the day, the same man was out at the dumpster unloading a bin full of trash. Only, no he wasn't, he was actually reading papers from an open trash bag. This is when I got the feeling of panic and not knowing what to do. JB says "Report him." I say, I have to live here for another 12 days after I report him and things already aren't going so well. Now I feel unsafe and a tad bit paranoid.

This morning sealed the deal. I was awakened at 6:30am by Indian music. Very loud Indian music. Ironic, isn't it? Yesterday, my aunt said that God has a good sense humor. Boy, she wasn't kidding. I pulled out the phone book and called the Marriott Residence Inn. I told them I would take anything they had, I would even sleep in their lobby. I said, "Hear that Indian music?"

"Yes", she said.

"That music is not coming from *my* room."

"*Oh!*"

"Uh-huh."

One the other side of the world...JB had a feeling that he probably shouldn't ask for a tour of the cafeteria where he works. Now he's the one feeling slightly panicky!

License to Steal

I didn't know the specifics about hotel laws and had never noticed them (or read them) in a hotel room. I was informed today that in the state of Illinois, a hotel is only liable for $250.00. Even if it's the hotel's fault that over $3000.00 worth of goods were stolen from your room.

Doesn't that mean that the hotel staff can do whatever they want, even steal whatever they want without that staff member, or the hotel for that matter, having to take any responsibility for it? The hotel doesn't care. An insurance payout of $250.00 is no big deal to them in the grand scheme of things.

Personally, I think these *laws* are a license to steal. I thought laws were passed for the purpose of order and protection. These particular laws protect criminals and then there's nobody to be held accountable. How nice for them.

Bittersweet Labor

Some of you may be able to follow me on this one...

Remember the first time you were pregnant? About 8 months or so along, you start to worry what labor will be like but there's no turning back. You know it's going to be really uncomfortable, however at that point, you have no choice but to just go through it. You're looking forward to the baby and dreading what the unknown labor pain will be like.

OK, that's how I'm feeling about India today.

Responsibility and *accountability* are defined in the Webster's Dictionary as follows:

> Main Entry: re·spon·si·bil·i·ty 1Pronunciation: ri-"spän(t)-s&-'bi-l&-tE
> Function: noun
> Inflected Form(s): plural -ties1 : the quality or state of being responsible2 : as
> a : moral, legal, or mental accountability
>
> b : RELIABILITY3, TRUSTWORTHINESS42 : something for which one is responsible5
> Main Entry: ac·count·abil·i·ty 6Pronunciation: &-"kaun-t&-'bi-l&-tE
> Function: noun
> the quality or state of being accountable7;
> especially : an obligation or willingness to accept responsibility or to account8 for one's actions

Some people only take responsibility for their actions when they're backed into a corner. And believe me, some even refuse to be held accountable when all fingers are pointing at them and there's no room to wiggle in that corner they're crouched into. I'm not a big fan of confrontation but I will stand my ground when I know I'm right...yes, I admit that sometimes I am wrong. I was getting so sick of people crying, "I didn't doooooooooo it."

Unfortunately, push came to shove with the moving company but at least they're now willing to pay the expense of shipping our overflow. Initially, they told our relocation coordinator that I moved a ton (2300lbs +) of inventory off our storage list into our shipment. I moved one desk. I also took plenty off the shipping list and moved it into storage. I requested to see a detailed list of the items that I supposedly added to our shipment. JB's letter was more harsh than mine.

Now we're getting the 'I didn't really do it but I'll take responsibility for it' song. My interpretation of that is, 'I know we screwed up and we'll take responsibility for it since we don't want to lose our fat contract when you explain to your employer why you're asking them to foot the bill for our $8000 mistake.'

It's a mean to an end. It's one small step for mankind in the accountability department.

And so, I'm off to pack up our hotel room. There will definitely be a surplus of luggage accompanying us to India on Friday. I anticipate that I'll have the responsibility of paying for extra luggage since I'm the only one that can be held accountable for packing my own suitcases. See how that works?

Saree We're Leaving

Today was the height of our yay-boos. I dropped Kramer off at the kennel and finished up all the last minute stuff to prepare him to be shipped. I hate leaving my pooch. It's like walking away from a crying baby. It will be a long two weeks with no furry tummy wummy to scratch.

Connor had a going away party at school this morning. We treated the class to a pizza lunch. They tried to tied him up to prevent him from leaving. He started to get very emotional so I suggested we get ourselves together enough for a quick hand wave goodbye on our way out of the room. He did great. Then the whole class followed him out into the hallway and gathered around him for a 23 person bear hug. By that time, I was sobbing behind my sunglasses.

We went out to the car and we cried our hearts out. It just tore me up to see him so upset. We agreed we would sit there and cry as long as we wanted and then we were going to be really happy to get on that plane to go see Dad.

On the other end of the emotional scale, I'm so excited to just get going. I've been spinning my wheels long enough these past few weeks in Illinois and I'm just rea-dy. I'm sad to leave friends but I know that some will keep in touch no matter where I live. That makes it easier to go.

Things have been so crazy this week so I'm 'saree' if I haven't replied to emails. I will though...from India. Connor had the choice to go anywhere for dinner and he's chosen McDonald's. I'm off for one last burger. See you from the other side!

Welcome to Ch...

Chicago. I bet you thought I was going to say Chennai. Sometimes you just have to laugh at your circumstances, chocolate helps. A big shout-out to my friend Penny who packed me and Connor treat bags well stocked with chocolate.

To sum up the day; delay, delay, delay, sat on the runway for more delay, missed flight, standby, no flight, full flights, hotel and hopefully a flight tomorrow. Insert plenty of rain, heavy bags, $387 surcharge for a suitcase 4lbs over the limit, lots of lines, changing terminals, waiting, frustrated airline employees, a $6 tube of toothpaste and a 10 year old. OK, here's the bottom line...sitting on the runway for 30 minutes extended our trip an additional 24hours. So, doubling it.

And, two guys that had worked for JB before he went to India were on my flight into Chicago. They both got onto flights to Chennai and will actually get to see him before I do.

I've kept my sense of humor. I didn't freak. I haven't screamed at anyone (including Connor). I've even been patient. And Connor has truly been a *trooper!*

Tonight, we indulged ourselves with Chicago pizza. Might as well make the best of it, right? We're going to try again tomorrow. I hope we have enough chocolate to get us through.

Seriously.

First Post From Chennai

Wow.

Fascinating and Overwhelming

Our first day in India was fascinating and overwhelming.

We woke up early and stared out the window for hours. I'm not kidding, we couldn't tear ourselves away. Inside the gate of the hotel is a lush tropical paradise...palm trees, colorful plants, interesting birds, good food and eager staff.

On the other side of the gate is a world that I doubt I could describe. Just when I think I've seen the most fascinating and peculiar thing ever, I see something even more fascinating. Am I using the word 'fascinating' too much? Like I said, I don't believe I have the words yet.

We went by the house yesterday to check on the progress. We met our landlord and I think we lucked out in that department. He appears to be a man who does what he says he'll do without any bull. The pool is in and being backfilled by three or four women carrying bowls of dirt on their heads, barefoot across uneven ground, while their children look on. I don't believe anyone from a culture laden with convenience would feel good watching this scenario. When we talked about it later, JB explained that bringing in a skid steer loader, or even a wheel barrow, meant these women would be out of work and their families would have no income.

We went to the mall to buy sheets for our temporary beds. After being stared at and chased down to buy lipstick, jet lag began affecting my thought process. We decided the day had been overwhelming enough. Just watching India out our hotel room window had been overwhelming. Am I using the word 'overwhelming' too frequently? We came back to the hotel for a nap and dinner.

Over the next few days when I'm a little more rested, I'm really looking forward to going plant shopping with the landlord's wife. She's going to let me choose some of the plants for the landscaping and the window boxes. We may take a drive by the school to see where it is. We'd also like to find a place to fly Connor's cool new dragon kite that JB got for him in China. I'm excited to meet a few families that I've been chatting with online about Chennai. And, on the weekend we'll be attending the company's Family Day outing.

This morning, I can hear the traffic picking up. I'm looking forward to taking some photos before the sights on the streets become normal routine to me. I know I'll want to just watch the hustle and bustle again today. Fascinating stuff.

An Auspicious Day

Today was an "auspicious" day. JB attended a Puja (See http://en.wikipedia.org/wiki/Puja) at the factory for the opening of a new gate. Another Puja was held by a supplier where they broke ground for a new facility. The third Puja took place at our new house, which included a fire pit in the middle of our living room, leaves and flowers on the front doors and designs of rice flour on the ground (to feed the ants). Because it was an auspicious day, our appliances were delivered today instead of yesterday.

Yesterday, however, there was a break down in communication with our driver. After he dropped us off at the hotel for lunch I told him we were done for the day. At 7pm, JB arrived at the hotel and asked why Driver Guy was still here. He had waited at the hotel for seven hours. Today went a little better, I wrote down the addresses of where I wanted to go and that seemed to help.

We trekked to the mall today to pre-order the next Harry Potter book. We also bought a tourist guide to India. Speaking of books, JB gave me a book to read entitled *Games Indians Play* by V. Raghunathan. It's a book that attempts to help people understand the "Indianess of Indians"... his words, not mine. I'm only a few pages in but it's interesting.

We had a Lebanese lunch at Cedars Restaurant with new friends. We went back to their house for a bit so the kids could play. Then we went by our house to have a peek at the progress. The women were carrying 10 bricks at a time on their heads. You should see how they load 'em on... it's so incredible! I'd totally drop all ten on my toes.

Tonight, I had a couple of cravings for:

1) Salad that wouldn't make me sick.

2) Ice tea that wasn't made using Indian water or ice...so we went to Sparky's (http://www.sparkysindia.com/). We were assured that the vegetables were washed with bottled water. The ice cubes were also made with bottled water. The lemonade was homemade. Oh! And for all my Canadian peeps...I even had poutine. We came away with full tummies for about $20 and a new church to boot. The owner is a Christian and gave us a couple of recommendations for non-denominational churches and an invitation to a Christian concert.

On our way back to the hotel tonight I was blown away by the sheer number of people out and about. There is far more traffic and bustle in the evenings than during the day. I have a better understanding of why we're not allowed to drive here. I know that I wouldn't likely leave the house if I had to drive myself.

Connor is taking India in stride and has surprised me how he's going with the flow. He says he misses his friends from his old school but earlier today he said, "I could get used to living in India." That was the highlight of my auspicious day.

A Few Tidbits

This will all be pretty random so it will be in point form...

- There are cows tied up on the sidewalk right outside the mall. And no, I don't think they're available for purchase, but I don't know it for sure. Picture a shopping mall on the street corner. There's no such thing as parking lots here so as we pull in to park in the underground parking, there are cows to the left and to the right. We had to surrender our bags as we entered each shop.

- I received what I thought was a very good tip to have our pantry air conditioned. I couldn't wait to ask my landlord about it before it was too late. She told her husband about it while I was standing there in such a way that made it sound like the craziest thing on earth. He just rolled his eyes and gave a "hmph." I'm thinking no air conditioning in our pantry. But I think I did score some extra upper cabinets in the kitchen. They think I'm silly for storing informal and formal dishes in the kitchen, and a remark was made about the amount of entertaining I must do like it was a bad thing. And we don't even entertain all the much but I'm sure she thinks we're party animals.

- Let's go back to the driver. This is a whole new thing for me and I like not having to maneuver my way around Chennai but I really don't like having a driver. I don't plan ahead, that's my problem. I don't ever plan ahead for a hair cut, I just show up. I don't plan if I need the driver tomorrow, but tomorrow a need to go somewhere might arise. Last night, I knew I didn't have any plans for today. JB asked Driver Guy to be here in the morning. Then I got a phone call asking if I planned to go anywhere, which I thought I'd clearly established the night before. The driver went home and made a trip/hung out at the hotel for nothing. See, I feel badly about that. JB says, "That's what he gets paid to do." I need more time to adjust.

- Sweeping is a profession. Many people are employed to sweep all day long. We're not talking about the same kind of brooms we know, these brooms don't have handles and are short. So far, I've only seen women sweepers and they use very short brooms that require them to bend over.

- They hotel staff knocked on my door twice, called me once and slipped a note under our door to ask if I was satisfied with our room--and that was just today. I'm very satisfied but would like to be left alone.

- I took the "bull by the horns" today and created an online forum for the company expat wives. I figure at the rate the company is sending families over here, women will need support and be a resource to one another. Now we just have to rely on our husbands to pass on the information about it.

- I've eaten Indian food about 50% of the time. There are buffets three times per day at the hotel and I've been trying not to order continental food from the menu. Indian food consists mainly of rice, meat or veg sauces to put over the rice and deep fried chicken or veg, varying from mild to screaming hot. The desserts are impressive but I've been good and have stayed away (well, mostly).

- Our hotel room toilet seat is square and very narrow. I equate it to sitting down after the seat has been left up. It requires some balance. TMI? Well, too bad, you're reading this blog for the info, aren't ya?

- The weather has been sunny and 93 degrees F every day. Every afternoon we go to the pool. Connor swims and I sit in the shade. I'm just not brave enough to wear a swimsuit at the hotel pool. I think I'll keep that horror for the privacy of our own pool.

- I've taken photos of entire families sitting on a moving motor bike. One or two kids in the front or the back. Women sit side-saddle on the back, often carrying their babies in their arms. Other modes of transportation are 5 people squeezed into a rickshaw, taxi cabs of the Harry Potter Ambassador variety, and the public bus system where they are so packed in that people hang off the sides. I've never really been a public transit kind of girl and wondered what these busses would be like in the rain since there are no windows.

- I definitely haven't packed enough bug spray. The Avon stuff is no match for the bugs here. If you're reading this and are planning any type of care package during our three years here, those would be good items to pick up when they're available in your area. Also, I wouldn't say no to "After-Bite" sticks.

- So far, none of us have felt sick from the food or any other cause. That surprises me, I expected to have felt rotten at least twice by now.

- I'm still very tired and can't seem to get day and night sorted out. Tonight, Connor fell asleep on the dinner table. I took photos but probably won't have them developed for a little while.

- We heard the Radisson Hotel has a good American poolside BarBQ so we may try that on Friday night.

- Television episodes from ABC and NBC are not viewable over the internet from India. I've purchased season passes for all my favorites on iTunes and will download them to my iPod. I'm thinking watching TV in the car might be a good distraction.

- Our air shipment is in Delhi but JB had to surrender his passport to obtain a Chinese visa for his next trip, so we can't claim our shipment. Our sea shipment is somewhere between LA and Singapore.

- JB is having the hotel tailor make him some pants that fit. He's lost so much weight from running that he looks terminally ill in his work clothes. Apparently, a trip to the tailor is how most people purchase their clothes. At the same time, we're having some of Connor's school uniforms cut into shorts. I messed up when packing his bags. I packed school uniforms and gym clothes. I thought our air shipment would be here before us so I put all his summer clothes in the shipment. Right now, he's dressing like it's winter or like he's a scrub. He's still cute though.

-JB's already talking about hosting 'a thing' once we're into the house. Bless his heart. I'm not hosting anything until every last box is unpacked and every last photo is on the wall.

- I'm so ready to move into our house so I can have a vacation. There will be no rush in unpacking those boxes.

Kramer: Globe Trotter

There is plenty to post about but the best news is that Kramer arrived in Chennai at 4:30am this morning. It was our first night in the house and none of us slept well. It will take a little while to get used to the hustle and bustle here, even in the middle of the night, such as dump trucks unloading sand in our yard at midnight and horns honking to be let in the gate.

We were up half the night waiting on Kramer. We kept looking out the window to see if they were at the gate. Hopefully, the guards didn't think we were spying on them. But, we did that too just to see what they were up to in the middle of the night.

I was so excited when the truck pulled up! I threw on flip-flops and ran out to see Kramer. Then I realized that I had embarrassed the guards by running out in the street in my jammies. Ha! Wait 'til I walk out to the pool in a swimsuit boys. I poured the dog a liter of water and he drank the whole thing. I poured another liter of water and he slurped that up too. Then he crashed. He's exhausted from the trip.

Kramer is enjoying all the attention today from the landlord, pool guy, sweeper, driver, guards and other miscellaneous people roaming around here today. He went for a drive to the grocery store with us. The driver kept the air conditioner running for him but he had to take away the box of tissue. Naughty pooch.

I love that stinkin' mutt. I'm so glad he's here with us!

Family Day

Before I get into Family Day, let me back up a few days.

I thought if I could get one good night of sleep, I could snap my body into the right time zone. I took a sleeping pill and slept well. And, I slept most of the following day because the pill was too strong for me. So, the vicious cycle continues. A nap feels so good and it's so hard to open my eyes! I've been having some pain under my ribs on the right side and running a low grade fever for the past couple of days. I've tried a few various home remedies but, so far, nothing has worked. I may have to take a pop to the doc to have it checked out if I get fed up enough over the next few days.

That said, today was Family Day at Queensland Amusement Park (http://www.queenslandamusementpark.com/) with 3000 people attending. I wasn't sure if I was going to go because I had been awake most of the night praying for relief. I really felt bad missing JB's first official 'thing' so I went. It was a very hot 95°F and felt hotter with the humidity. With the low grade fever I was sweating, feeling dizzy, queasy and all around miserable. But I did it without vomiting or passing out, so I reached the goal!

Today, the previous managing director was retiring and JB was officially taking over. A few speeches were made, mostly in Tamil. Then JB and Old MD Guy said a few words that were translated. They were both given large glass display cases that held a statue of Nataraj, lord of Dance (http://www.lotussculpture.com/nataraj1.htm), saffron-colored silk wraps around their shoulders as a sign of respect, and long ornate sandalwood beads with medallions around their necks.

Generally, I'm fairly secure person so the amount of staring and pointing didn't bother me. I understand that for some people, especially the ones that live in small villages, they rarely see white skin, blond hair or blue eyes. Many people wanted to meet JB. It was an honor for them to have their families meet the boss. And it was an honor for us to meet their families too. They brought their children to shake hands with us. We were actually asked to sign autographs. And even some people who weren't affiliated with the company came over to take our photos or to take our photos with their children. Total strangers were kissing on Connor's cheeks. I can't help it either, I understand the draw of those marshmallow cheeks but he was really freaked out!

The highlight of my day was a little girl around the age of 2 whose parents wanted her to pose for a picture with me. She was scared of me and she didn't understand what I was saying to her. She looked so sweet with her little pierced ears and gold bangle on her wrist. Finally, her parents got the photo and when her mom picked her up I noticed that she was wearing a cross on a chain around her neck. I pointed to her cross and then I pointed to my cross so I could show her that I wore a cross too. Another woman said, "Jesus, Jesus." I nodded my head. The little girl smiled, she understood the name Jesus.

By this time, Connor and I had just about as much heat as we could take. We didn't go on any rides and I stayed under the umbrella I brought with me. Among the stares, a few groups of girls pointed to my umbrella and my Keds shoes, giggling. Hey, a fair girl like me needs to bring her own shade and comfortable footwear. There were only a few brief seconds that it made me feel little insecure but I got over it quickly chalking it up to fact that *we* are what's different in this picture.

I was very pleased when I returned to the hotel and received an invitation to visit a tailor this week to have a few Salwar Kameez sets made (a long tunic, pants and scarf). The next function, such as a family day, I'll definitely wear the Indian garb to save myself a few stares and a few insecurities. Connor is excited, he wants a say in the fabric I pick. So how about that? I just moved here, and I'm going shopping with the girls!

Staff Stuff

We had a lovely Easter and turkey dinner with our new American friends on Sunday. It was a nice respite from what was otherwise a cruddy weekend. Hopefully, we'll be getting our food shipment today. We have a very busy day planned but I'll tell you about it another time.

Staff. Help or headache? Having household staff is a completely new thing for me. There are many people around the house on any given day, especially with the extra workers still doing the brick work and landscaping out in the yard.

We had to get a new driver. Our first driver didn't speak English. When he found out that we had requested a new driver, he said, "You say, I go. Yes?" Yes. But, he couldn't help me when people were showing up at the house and I didn't know who they were or why they were here. When I tried to explain to him that he was a very good driver and we like him very much, but we really need someone with more English. He said, "No Understand." Exactly my point.

Which brings me to the guards. They didn't speak English either. My Tamil in nonexistent. So they weren't able to tell me who was coming and going either.

One night we had a meeting at the house with the car and security people. We were assured that we would be given a driver who speaks English and, in the future, all security guards would speak English. I told them I would be happy if I could communicate with at least one guard per shift.

So, our new driver, Prabheesh, not only speaks English, but apparently he's very obedient too. Prabheesh drove us to the grocery store the other day. When we arrived, he jumped out of the truck to open our doors. I said to Kramer, "Stay." And Prabheesh, who was midway out of his door, jumped back into the car and sat. Connor and I couldn't help but laugh, we meant for the dog to stay.

Last night, I woke up at 5am and decided I would come upstairs to check email. The "MD" (as all the staff refers to JB) left for Beijing at 9pm. I looked out the window to the gate and the guard was sleeping on the guardhouse step. I went outside with Kramer and walked around the pool so I could see well into the guardhouse. A second guard was sleeping at the table. While we wandered around outside, they didn't even wake up. Finally the third guard came out from from behind the house and woke them up. While the MD's away, I guess they don't have to guard the house? Hmmmm.

Today, our housekeeper cum cook will start work. Her Hindu name is Jayanthi but she asked us to call her by her Christian name, Roslen. She was the only person that we interviewed that didn't seem petrified of Kramer and she used to work for the German Consular General. Oh, and she'll cook meat, which most people understandably won't do if they don't eat it.

I think it will take me a while to get the hang of this.

Follow up note: Our housekeeper/cook cannot leave her current position until they find a replacement for her. She suggested I hire her sister. Her sister had come with her to the interview and was afraid of our dog. So, I said, "Forget it." No housekeeper for now.

Week of Firsts

Who's on first? Just kidding, it was a week of firsts!

- Our first swim (JB and me) in our swimming pool.

- Our first trip to Connor's school. The guidance counselor took us for our appointment an hour late and we only had 15 minutes to spare before having to run to the Immigration office to register.

- Our first trip to the Immigration office. After hearing horror stories about this place it went very smoothly. I know if I were attempting that process on my own, it would've been ugly.

- Connor's first day of school in India. He's in 5th grade and likes his teacher, although she's no Mrs. Diggle! I'm not sure who was more nervous, him or me!

- Connor's first math test on the first day of school. It was a wash out. He was too nervous and completely freaked out when he saw the metric system. He brought it home for homework instead.

- My first long day alone in India. I couldn't hack it. I went over to a friend's house to scope out her scrapbook pages. I was very grateful for the distraction and very impressed by her pages.

- My first outing to the appliance stores in search of dehumidifiers. Apparently, they don't exist here. Today, my new driver took me to a very busy street. The kind of street I'd previously only had driven by. *gulp*

- I just noticed at least 6 very large tree stumps in the middle of the street on our way back from school. I'm talking about swerving to miss a tree stump as we're driving down the road. It looks like the trees were chopped down with 6" of the stump being left. Then the road was just paved around it. The ones I've seen out in the middle have barricades near them forcing people to drive around them. The ones closer to the curb are just, well...watch where you're driving. I'm sure one day I'll see a bicycle or motorbike flip into the air after slamming into them.

- My first time buying vegetables in India. And soaking them in food purifier so we can actually eat them without getting sick.

- Our first time paying $22.00 for a bottle of Parmesan cheese. I won't tell you what the beer cost.

- My first time interviewing people for the purpose of hiring them. Actually, I'm gaining experience in this area, although I still haven't hired anyone. That probably makes me sound picky. I'm actually not. As they say, good help is hard to find.

- My first week of really 'roughing it.' I've had better amenities when I've been camping. I'm not complaining, I'm just saying when you can't open your can of tuna because you don't have a can opener...

- Geckos. I've swept two of them out of the house after they scared the daylights out of me, screaming like a wimpy girl all the while. That's me squealing, not the geckos. They took it like the brawny little lizards that they are. Yeah, yeah, I know, they eat mosquitoes. Let them eat mosquitoes outside. *shiver*

- We watched grass being planted here for the first time. Three blades of grass plugged into the ground about 6" apart for the whole "lawn." I use the term "lawn" very loosely because it looks like muddy hair plugs.

- I just caught the new security guard looking into the bedroom window. When he realized the glass was frosted, he made his way to the back door where we came face to face. I wasn't spying on him. I was looking out the window while I was taking the sheets out of the drier. I opened the door and told him he had no business looking in our windows. "I just go," he said pointing back and forth to indicate that he was just guarding the back yard. Uh huh. While the snooping guard was a first at our house, so was it a first for me to go out to the gate ranting and raving like a crazy lady. MD wife crrrrrazy. Oh yea, I'm feeling a little punchy tonight.

- Tomorrow, I'm taking my first trip to the nursery for a little plant shopping with my landlady so the landscaping and window boxes can be finished.

What a week. I'm looking forward to our first weekend of just chilling out and JB's first birthday in India!

Death in the Street of Chennai

I had a very busy day. I attended the school PTA meeting, hung out with a friend, went out to lunch--Thai, yum! I came back to an array of issues regarding intercom systems, telephones, a swampy-green swimming pool, more geckos (and more girlie squealing...this time it was JB) and at least four hours of homework. Let me back up. The homework came after a few tears, a discussion with Connor's teacher AND him begging me to homeschool him. It wasn't a good day for him. He came home feeling inferior in art, stupid in math and frustrated that so many languages are being spoken in the classroom all at the same time. I think we'll get that all worked out but that's not why I'm posting.

You just wouldn't have believed the scene on my way to pick up Connor at school today! I was listening to an iPod with noise-reduction headphones (getting my God on) so I really didn't see what was happening until I was nearly right on top of it all. I noticed there were flowers all over the street. Then I noticed that we weren't moving freely in traffic. I asked Prabheesh (my driver) why there were flowers everywhere and he pointed to what looked like a parade float. It was being wheeled through the street with a dead body laying on it. The body was covered with flowers and more flowers were being thrown into the street while throngs of people milled around it and played drum-like instruments. Some sang. Some drank. This is the tradition of death in the state of Tamil Nadu. I could only find this link to provide a little more information: http://www.webindia123.com/tamilnadu/People/death.htm

As disrespectful as it would've been, I would have loved to have taken photos of this scene. I was also sorry Connor wasn't with me to see it because he certainly didn't believe much of how I described it.

Interestingly enough, this all led to a conversation with Prabheesh about how he's from another state with different traditions. I asked if his wife and children live in Chennai or Kerala. He informed me that he isn't married. He is also the sole provider for his parents and two brothers. He wears a wedding band, but says, "No, that's just fashion." A woman, though, shows she's married by wearing a ring on a certain toe on each foot. Well, then I just couldn't resist toying with him. "What if the woman is wearing shoes instead of sandals? How do you know she's married then?" Oh Danie, just stop!

Happy Birthday JB!

On Saturday, Connor and I went shopping at Spencer Plaza. Before we went to the mall, I did a little shopping over the internet. At the mall, we bought JB a replacement video iPod since his was stolen back in Illinois. When I tried to buy him flip-flops for the pool, my debit/check card was declined. Just as I'm handing a different card to sales clerk, my phone rings. It's JB, in Beijing, his card won't work either. Due to there having been transactions in three countries within a couple of hours, the bank red-flagged our card (assuming it was stolen) and froze our cash. So, JB had birthday presents for his birthday, but we didn't get to buy any gift wrap. Our bank has "hometown" hours. So it was a bit of a chore to get a hold of someone and get our cards back to normal...KA-ching!

I baked my first cake in India and it didn't go so well. Looking back at it now, it's pretty funny. I bought a bundt cake pan at a local store. It turns out; this pan isn't as deep as our American variety. The cake started to rise and pour over the sides into the oven. Then the drippings caught on fire. Did I mention that I have a gas oven? Fire is probably not a good thing. I took the cake out of the oven, scraped the top off, poured some batter out and put it back in the oven. Now I wasn't sure how long to cook it. I also used butter instead of oil. I had to improvise not only on the cake but the whole birthday celebration. Oh well! I was wearing my Girl Scout hat. Not the one that said "Be Prepared," the one that said, "Adapt and Overcome." Wait, is that the military? Well, you know what I mean.

JB was happy. He was impressed that we even managed to surprise him with gifts. The man hates a fuss being made over him but as if I wouldn't celebrate the day that God put him on this earth for me to love.

We had a meeting with our security guards and their supervisor. We asked for more privacy and for Connor to be called by name (not "Master"). We asked that they allow Connor to do his chores and carry trash out to the bin. Can you imagine the kind of rotten child that lands back in the US after getting used to being called Master and not doing chores? Ick. Their requests were quite reasonable but may be a little more difficult to make happen.

By the end of the day we were all exhausted. We picked a restaurant that opened early so we wouldn't have to wait until 7pm (like most restaurants). We went back to Le Meridien. All in all, JB had a nice birthday and we were pleased to have made the first family birthday in India a success.

Ashraya Something or Other

Today was Ashraya something or other. Sorry, I've forgotten the second word. It was an auspicious day to buy jewelry. More specifically, I've just been told, to buy white jewelry. In doing so, wealth and luck will come one's way. Or something. As JB says, I don't need an auspicious day to purchase jewelry! I went with a friend to a huge jewelry multi-level galleria. In fact, we went to two massive shops. I was good, I bought silver so I didn't spend too much. I had my eye on a few platinum bangles with bling but they were made for emaciated people with money. I would tell everyone about the pieces I bought, but I can't. I mostly bought gifts. Shopping sure does work up an appetite, so we just had to go out to lunch, right?

This might seem silly--and some may say superficial. It is what it is. There a few things that gauge how quickly I've settled in to a new place. We've moved so much that I actually have a system for this! There are three steps:

1. There are names on mobile phone call list.

2. My days are busy.

3. I run into people I know when I'm out and about.

Usually, number one happens quickly. But two and three take more time. Sometimes, it takes months. In India, all three of these things have happened in less than 4 weeks. That's definitely a new record for me. While we were at lunch today, I ran into two people that I know. It makes me feel settled and like I'm beginning to belong here.

On my way home from school this morning I had a *moment*. Well, a moment or a feeling. Call it what you like. I felt like for whatever reason, this is where I'm supposed to be right now. I have no idea what God's plan is for me, and I never do. But I do believe I'm where I'm meant to be. I hope I still feel that way during the coming months and years. I believe it's this calmness that has gotten me through all the ups and downs of this move. Bring it on, I can handle it.

A couple of tidbits of good news...maybe it really is an auspicious day…

- I'm not sure if I mentioned that the basement in our IL house flooded this week. As it turns out, the sump pump gave out and the entire carpet in the basement and stairs must be replaced. Where's the good news, you might be thinking. The good news is that while our house had to be taken off the market, my friend Penny and our realtor/friend Kelly have handled everything on our behalf. Penny is like the 8th wonder of the world when it comes to getting things done so I'm just not worried about it. Also, we shouldn't have to sign a new disclosure since it was the sump pump and not the foundation. Goooo Penny!

- Yesterday, we heard from the insurance agent that represents Extended Steal America and the claim has been settled. While it didn't come anywhere near the amount of the stolen property, the hotel made a goodwill gesture to pay about half. That's better than the $250 that we were previously entitled to.

- Our sea shipment has arrived in Chennai! I'm hoping to have it delivered before the weekend but hoping can lead to disappointment here. More realistically, I'm guessing we'll get it sometime next week but at least it's here. I can't wait to sleep in our own bed. I'm giddy with the thought.

- Sanjaya has been voted off American Idol! What more can a girl ask for?

Maybe buying jewelry on an auspicious day does grant good things!

I Miss IL today

Yesterday (Saturday) was a a day of errands. Once JB was done with work, we went shopping on East Coast Road (ECR). We bought some cane furniture to put on our front porch. I paid the asking price because it was such a good price I didn't even have the heart to barter for a better one. For two chairs, a sofa, coffee table, side table, all the cushions, glass table tops and delivery $193.00. Could I have gotten it cheaper? Yes. But we chose generosity.

We toodled around town checking out various shops for various items. Then we hit the mall last night because the Jelly Bean needed shoes. We got home and we were all exhausted. Including our driver who fell asleep today. He wanted overtime, we gave it to him.

In any other time or place it would take me months before I found and tried out a new church. Except here. In India I have found that having a driver has been the key to finding a friend's house even if I don't know the address or general location, finding a church that I would never have found if I were driving, or where to buy that specific thing. He'll take me there.

So with half directions to a nondenominational church we went to the early--shorter--service. I long for a church with at least a pastor. I liked the music today, though. The message was long and repetitive. It was delivered by a woman who used algebra and the third law of thermodynamics to make her point. Repeatedly. I'm serious.

There's another non-denominational church that we may try next week. I left the service today feeling sad. Missing our church in Illinois. A church that I knew was the perfect fit and knew I would likely never find one like it again. After church, we went to brunch. It was a veritable binge on carbs. Comfort food: pancakes, waffles, french toast, moussaka, tzatziki, hummus and ice tea.

We made an attempt to buy a fan today for the guardhouse. We stopped at a very long red light on our way to the shop. What happened next was something I had been told about but had not yet experienced. I hadn't expected it since we've lived here for a month and it hadn't happened. While we were stopped at the light, several people came to the car to sell us feather dusters, sun visors, cotton swabs and (what looked like) felt chamois cloths. That part I can deal with. When we didn't respond, they put their faces up to the windows, shading their eyes with their hands to see in through the tinted glass. Then the knocking started. They knocked repeatedly on the windows to get our attention. Then more people came to the windows. More knocking. I have to admit, I was a little nervous. At no time since we've moved here have I felt unsafe. I felt relieved when Prabheesh locked the car doors, though, because by that time I was completely freaked out and staring at JB like a gasping fish.

We came home without the fan. I'll try again tomorrow. As well as we've settled in, I guess it can be expected for us to have those "cultural moments" that throw us for a loop. The rest of day was spent napping, visiting friends and swimming. All's well that ends well.

Creepy Crawlies

It was so nice to have dinner with our friend, JB Senior, from Illinois this evening. Wonderful to see a familiar face and fun to hear his first impressions of India, knowing we didn't get it wrong. I said, "Can you believe we live here?" He was speechless. And he brought a suitcase full of goodies. So nice. That's not the creepy crawly part of my day though...

I was awake very early making phone calls to my mom, aunt and friend. I laid in bed chatting on the phone for a long time with my mom. Then I called my aunt. As I was chatting with her, I rolled over, moved my head and came face to face with a gecko. Literally, it was 6" from my face. I wonder if my poor auntie has regained her hearing yet?

When we got home from dinner last night, George was on duty. George is our foremost English speaking security guard. He takes great delight in giving me detailed reports of everything that goes on since he's really the only one who can. As we drove up the driveway, I could see George practically running behind the car. I knew he wanted to report something. While we were at dinner, a huge snake slithered off the roof and landed at the feet of one of the younger security guards. George even reported in detail about how the guard screamed, which made me laugh on the inside. Of course, he was dying to show me the snake because he had the honor of being the one to smash it's head with a stick. I say this with a bit of sarcasm because he's Christian. A Hindu would likely hold some type of religious ceremony after the snake was killed. George said it was a cobra, the driver, who looked annoyed by the whole thing, said it was a python. Granted, he was trying to identify it sans head. It was 5.5 to 6 feet long.

Can I just say how glad I am that I wasn't here for this whole scene?

When we got back inside, I turned JB into The Crocod...oops, I mean Gecko Hunter. He was ready to give up easily and allow me to sleep with Connor. There was no way I was going to bed with a gecko in my bedroom and I persisted that he extricate it from our sleeping quarters.

Surprisingly enough, I slept well last night. Perhaps it's because I know that I'll be sleeping in my very own bed tomorrow night!

Creepy Crawlies, Part II

It was definitely a cobra (http://en.wikipedia.org/wiki/Indian_Cobra).

The Hindu staff are upset today that the cobra wasn't burned. And then when it's burned a religious ceremony must take place afterwards. None of that happened. The dead cobra was gone from the rubbish pile this morning and they think it's still alive, has slithered off and will come back for revenge (http://www.wildlifesos.com/rprotect/snakemyths.htm).

The security guard noticed the shedded snake skin hanging from a tree yesterday afternoon. This was cause for concern and they were on the lookout for the cobra. Because our best English speaking guard wasn't on day shift yesterday, we weren't told about the concern.

I was actually standing right underneath that very tree yesterday morning with our landlords, trying to decide where the clothes line should go. I've now decided that if I need a clothesline, it's not going to be under the trees.

This morning, I was shown the snake skin hanging from the tree. Connor wanted to see it before school. A ladder appeared and McGyver--my new name for Prabheesh--came with a big stick. He broke a smaller one off the tree and wrapped a piece of plastic package tape around it to create a hook. He hooked the tree branch and got the snake skin for Connor. We even have the part of the snake skin that covered its head. McGyver says, "Definitely a cobra madame." Then added with a smile, "I know snakes."

My landlord was back today about the clothesline and laughed at me when I said I'd think about it. "Oh, it's just a snake," he says. Somehow, referring to a venomous cobra as "just a snake" is like calling a destructive tsunami a "little wave."

We have requested the guards to watch Connor if he's in any of the grassy areas. I was told that this is their duty but they didn't want to hover since we requested privacy. Good point. They also told me they would play with Connor which is not necessary. (I've since learned that playing with him is the guise for watching him.)

I hate to sound like a big weenie but the truth is, when it comes to venomous snakes and docile geckos; I am a big weenie.

Creepy Crawlies, Part III

Like a really cheesy horror flick, you had to know there would a part III! I'd love to label this "the last chapter" as if it were the final element to the story, but I have a feeling there will be many more posts about creepy crawlies.

The day after the cobra, I witnessed a guard pounding on the ground with brick. I observed for a few seconds and met him around the other side of the house as he was about to dispose of a "baby cobra." Where's there's one baby, there's generally 12 to 30 more.

It was suggested to me by two people (within about a half hour span) to call the Snake Park at Guindy National Park to request someone come out and round up any snakes on the property. It was also suggested that we have a Puja so that the Hindu staff can feel like my house's karma has been cleansed. Not a bad idea. I'm actually considering it.

Prabheesh made several phone calls to the snake people and the answer was "tomorrow." Tomorrow is a common answer here. It could mean next week or maybe even next month, but we don't want to disappoint you so we'll tell you tomorrow. Repeatedly. After a couple of tomorrows went by, I had Prabheesh call again. This time I had him tell them that the Canadian women was going to kill every snake she could find....better come quick. That would offend the person on the other end of the phone line if he were Hindu. The Hindu Snake Guy arrived within a half hour.

We watched Snake Guy from afar. He wasn't finding any snakes. Meanwhile, McGyver got a couple of mangos down from a tree in our backyard for us to try. I soaked them, cut them, tasted them, and promptly spit it out. They weren't ripe and were very sour. McGyver knows snakes, but mangos, not so much.

Snake Guy was screaming over by the generator/guardhouse. He found a snake and we all went running to watch from the driveway. It's the same kind of snake that had been killed the day before but it's not a baby cobra. It's a Common Krait[1] and apparently more deadly than any cobra. Don't the Creepy Crawlies posts get better and better?

After he catches the snake (very near where I usually catch the guards sleeping), JB arrived with our friend from Illinois. They both got to see the see the snake before it was carted off. I'm fairly certain he's going to have plenty of stories to tell his wife, Penny. I'm pretty sure she'll never come to visit now and she's possibly the only person that was going to visit in the first place. All bets are off with family, I'm sure. What seemed like a tropical vacation destination within our walls is now a snake park.

In other news, our sea shipment arrived in 7 truck loads this Wednesday. I slept in my own bed for the first time in two months. Connor is thrilled with his new furniture and is sleeping like a baby. Ten of the grimiest people I've ever seen unloaded the trucks. They were supposed to come back the next day to unpack/assemble but I asked them not to. We don't own fine things but they are *our* things. I'm sure nobody will be surprised to hear that many of our belongings were damaged and treated carelessly during this move. I just didn't want anything else to be handled. Also, the entire stairwell needs to be repainted because of the amount of dirt and scratches.

It will take a longer time to unpack and assemble furniture. Especially with JB's time being at a premium. Our house is an overwhelming sight of boxes. I'm told I'll need to be patient since it was I who told the movers not to come back. Manage, manage, manage...

I put a good dent into the kitchen and will continue to work on it today. As long as I get out of the house each day to feel a little normalcy, I'm ok :)

[1] Photo: http://www.flickr.com/photos/wildhiss/245522373/in/set-725322/

Info: http://en.wikipedia.org/wiki/Common_Krait)

Pondy Bazaar and Richie Street

Here are a few photos from a recent shopping trip. Pondy Bazaar is where the locals shop for just about anything. If it's not found somewhere in Pondy Bazaar, chances are you don't need it.

After Pondy Bazaar, we ventured over to Richie Street. This is a condensed area of electronics shops. We went back there this weekend to find a new wireless router. I stayed in the car with Connor while JB ran into the shop. We chatted with our driver while we waited--always interesting! He told us that he travels 18km each way to come to work. He has to wake up at 4am each day. He explained bits of the process of arranging a marriage, which his parents are likely to do for him in another 6 months or so. This is fascinating to me and fills me with horror at the thought of the person my parents would have likely matched me with 15 years ago. Eek!

The countdown is on...one month left of school! We're starting to plan a couple of summer time vacations. We *all need* a vacation!

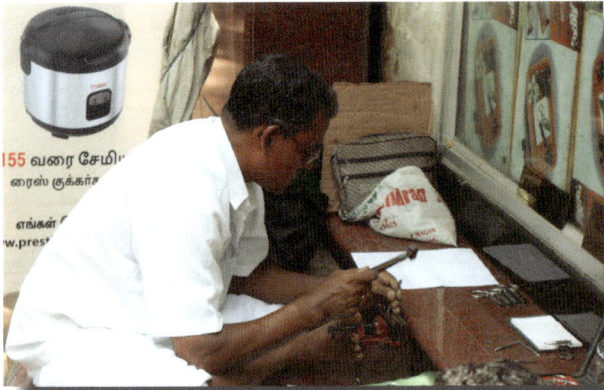

Engraver Guy

Aluminum Shop

Richie Street

Auto Rickshaw

Indian I.T.

OK, so I spent the whole weekend trying to set up our wireless network. I'm a big geek at heart, so this type of stuff is not usually a problem for me. I couldn't get it to work! JB suggested perhaps we need a new wireless router. We got a second router and still no luck.

I just spent an hour and a half on the phone with Indian IT-Girl. She walked me through all the stuff that I'd done before. Twice. The conversation was made much longer than necessary because of the extra non-IT talk:

Me: "Pardon?" "Excuse Me?" "Yes."

IT-Girl: "Tell Me." "Hello?" "Yes?" And repeating instructions slower for me to understand what she was saying.

Still, the wireless network is not working. It shows a full connection, yet we can't actually reach the internet. Her suggestion was that there is a problem with the wireless card in the laptop. Nice cop out when you can't solve the problem. My answer to that was...why is it, then, that we can connect to a certain European Consulate's unsecured wireless network next door (sorry boys...no wep key means free internet access for the whole neighborhood) but we can't connect to our own network? Anyone?

My evening was wasted and now I have to wait around tomorrow for IT-Guy to come to the house...sometime before 5pm. Don't you love that narrow window of about 8 hours?

In the meantime...To the boys next door, for Connor's many enjoyable hours of wireless Club Penguin, I'd just like to say, "Danke!" Appreciate it. Really.

Coconut-Guy

When we first moved to Chennai, our landlady told us that when we were ready she would arrange for a guy to come over, climb the trees and harvest the coconuts. I had never thought about how coconuts got to the ground but I'm pretty sure it involved shaking the tree or something equally as silly.

Coconut Guy scaled 10 trees like Spiderman. Actually, Spiderman wouldn't have been so fast or so agile. Spidy doesn't have a machete either. Come to think of it, Spider-man doesn't sound nearly as impressive as Coconut Guy.

As it turns out, we have four types of coconuts. We learned that the brown ones are to eat, the green ones are to drink and the orange ones are medicinal (especially mixed with rum, I was told).

George (head day guard) told us a story about the Hindu god Krishna and how he prevents people from getting hit on the head by falling coconuts. We made Kramer stay in the house though, just in case, until the coconuts stopped falling from the sky.

George (the poor guy was stung by a small scorpion while he was handling the branches), Prabheesh and Kasturi (the sweeper) all managed the cleanup and coconut distribution among the staff. We kept a few aside for JB and for our landlady.

As for the coconuts themselves... we tried the tender water warm, we tried it cold, and we don't want to try it again, warm or cold. Everyone thinks we're crazy. They love it. Kramer does too! He loved the smell and the taste. He drank two chilled glasses full. That dog is living large.

We really enjoyed this experience!

Mondays Are Fundays

The week began with another snake. Don't you just love Mondays? It was a Common Krait. By the time I was on my way to school, it was sans head. This time the staff burned it. Ew, barbecued krait before I had my morning caffeine. Later in the day, Snake Guy came out to do his thing. It only took one phone call and he came to the house the same day. Let me just stop right here to tell you how truly amazing that is in India. I'll drive that point home later in my Funday.

This was Snake Guy II, not the same Snake Guy that came the first time. Snake Guy II claims that he can smell the snakes. I think he was annoyed when I laughed at the translation of that. I thought he was kidding. Can humans really smell snakes out in the open? He was not kidding. He says there are no snakes living on our property (Thank You Jesus!) and that they're all finding our cushy expat property more pleasant than the overgrown, run-down, abandoned lot next door from which they come. There's good news in there somewhere.

Give a little love and it all comes back to you. Give a little coconut and that all comes back too. Everyone's wives and mamas are planning on cooking me coconut dishes. I was treated to coconut rice and vadam today by our head guard's wife. Her name is Savi, which is a shortened version of her very long name that I shamefully made a mess of pronouncing. I'm so relieved when people give me an easy Christian name or a shortened Hindu name.

"Savi means key in Tamil," gushed George. "She's the key to my lock." Cute. Stop. Savi insisted I eat some rice right away, which I did. It was delicious and I'm hoping to get the recipe so I can learn how to make at least one or two Indian dishes while we live here.

My mission today was to find brown paint and a paint brush. Next week is Book Week at school and the children will each be dressing up as a character in a book. This type of thing isn't like living in the US and being able to order something over the internet to have it arrive in time. This isn't even like being able to spend a couple of hours driving from store to store to obtain the necessary materials to create a character costume! As a friend said to me today, "We ain't in Kansas anymore!" We sure aren't! It wouldn't cost me $78 US dollars for a bit of brown acrylic paint and a paintbrush in Kansas! When Connor told his teacher that he would be dressing up as the "wardrobe" from *The Lion, The Witch and The Wardrobe*, her response was, "That's not a character." Well, it is now. I said so. Because I have lots of boxes and now I have expensive brown paint. His costume has to be something made out of a box and painted brown. Work with me lady!

The generator. There have been frequent power outages over the past few days. Our generator hasn't been kicking in automatically so the guards and drivers have been calling repeatedly to get it fixed. "Tomorrow." Ahh, the elusive *tomorrow*. I've gone through my landlady, my husband and the company. Generator Guy comes over and says the other Generator Guy needs to be the one to fix it. When can the other Generator Guy get here? You got it. Tomorrow. Repeat as necessary.

Here's the embarrassing part. Who on earth puts a cruddy no-name generator at the house of a generator-building company's MD? You would think we'd have a premium generator out there that kicked in automatically when the power fails. I haven't even tried to get the electrician out here yet to ensure that our pantry and bedroom A/C units come on automatically after a power reset or when we're on backup power. Tomorrow.

I had a terrific phone chat with our Clinical Case Worker this evening. She's the company-assigned person who checks in on us periodically to make sure we're coping alright with living abroad. I think we stayed on the phone way too long but I genuinely liked her and enjoyed chatted the evening away. She has a good sense of humor which I really needed tonight.

I'm glad Funday is over. It's too much "fun" for one person to handle alone in one day.

Negative Nelly

I think I'm going to become a vegetarian! Good animal flesh is hard to find here, especially of the oink and moo varieties. On our way to school yesterday we saw at least 20 chickens hanging upside down by their feet around the seat of a motorcycle. I wish I had my camera! The motorcycle was driving down the highway with us side-by-side. I was really grossed out when a couple of chickens began flapping their wings...they were alive! Total 'veg' dinner last night. I couldn't bring myself to eat any 'cluck' again today.

Speaking of food...It's my single most difficult adjustment to life in India. Cooking a meal is difficult. Getting the ingredients requires shopping at multiple stores. I'm not talking about Kroger, Sam's Club and Target either! Small, crowded over-heated shops that take a long time to get to, only to find out that they don't have what I'm looking for. It's very time and energy consuming. Especially in 110°F heat. As for cooking, I dread it. The kitchen is at the back of the house. This is normal in an Indian-style house because it's usually the housekeeper and/or cook to spend the most time in there, not the madame. Cooking back home meant I was in the same room as my family with the music or TV on. Cooking here means I'm alone at the back of the house and I can't hear or see anything, or anyone.

I brought some Salwar Sets to the tailor to be sewn into identifiable pieces of clothing. It was somewhat humiliating having my measurements called out in front of my friends. I tried to pretend I was anywhere else than where I was. La, la, la, I can't hear you. That night, I surfed the internet getting ideas for Indo-Western Salwar Kameezes. More Western, less Indo. To give you an idea, each set (tunic, pants and scarf) cost me about $10, and an additional $4 for the tailor to sew it to my exact measurements. $14 per outfit. How nuts is that?

A tantrum has been had. There's anger, pouting and avoidance. I'm talking about our head guard, King George, and not our 10 year old son. While I was in the middle of interviewing a housekeeper/cook, he informed me--yes, I said informed--that there was going to be a party on Sunday to celebrate his son's promotion after completing his bomb-squad training. It's also Savi's birthday (his wife). His grandchildren are coming and there was going to be cake to honor "master and beautiful madame". After I finished up with Mani (she's hired!), I started reeling about this party. At my house?! Did this mean I merely had to hangout at the gate for a few minutes to break cake with the staff? Or, was the intention for this party to take place in my house? What was expected of me in terms of the promotion of someone that we don't employ, and how about the guard's wife's birthday. Blurred lines and liberties was all I could think of. I sought the advice of friends and came to the realization that I had to back-peddle my way out of this or there were only bigger liberties that would be taken in the future. I went out to tell the guard that, "About Sunday...I'm sorry, sir said no."

"Sir" is such a meanie. I'm so glad "Sir" bails me out when I get myself in too deep! God bless the person who is "Sir." King George has avoided me and hasn't said two words to me since. Big baby.

Today was teacher appreciation day at school. Flowers, paintings and other niceys were given to the teachers as a way to say thank you. Special efforts were made for the teachers who are leaving the school. I don't know who the room mother is for Connor's class but I didn't know of anything that was being done for his teacher. That's probably because most people want to give her a shove out the door with their foot as she leaves. I tried to talk to her after school about the middle school band instrument selection and Connor's missing yearbook to no avail. One more thing, if a teacher is speaking rudely to your kid in front of you, chances are it's even worse when you're not around. I'd like to be the first to stand in line with my foot extended as she leaves the school. She is everything I dislike about teachers and the institution of school. She's everything I feared for Connor when I put him in school...a big bully. Because he had such a caring teacher in Illinois, he knows the difference and comes home daily with horror stories. Every day he's deflated and feels defeated. Why people like that are allowed to teach children and destroy their self-esteem daily is beyond me. I truly regret not staying in Peoria until the end of the school year for Connor's sake. It will be a long summer to erase his feelings about school and to convince him that 6th grade will be better. If I'm unsuccessful, homeschooling may be in our future. A tough way to spend three years in India. We'll have to determine what the lesser of the two evils will be.

As you can see from this post, I may be entering my Negative Nelly phase. Or, what I also call Stinkin' Thinkin.' On most days I have a positive outlook and I don't sweat the little stuff. I usually don't even sweat the big stuff of life in India. So, pardon my negativity, but it helps to get it off my chest so I can move on. Blogging is therapeutic, except for those who end up reading it.

Last Week of May

Last Friday was the Book Character day at school. As I had mentioned in a previous post, Connor's costume was going to have to be something fairly easy to make with what we had on hand, or rather, what we had already unpacked. He was the wardrobe from *The Lion, the Witch an the Wardrobe*. The wardrobe is a character? Maybe not, technically. But it's what I could manage. His teacher had previously "suggested" that he have a different costume. I asked Connor if his teacher said anything about his costume when he got to school. No, she just rolled her eyes at me. The character parade in the gym was very cute, although I think the books were chosen to go with whatever Halloween costumes people had on hand. The parade set off the mystery of the missing library book that Connor was supposed to hold up during the parade.

The beginning of the week was filled with tears, consoling, counselling and more tears. Connor is having such a rough go with his teacher. To make matters worse for him, there's a girl that has been goading him endlessly. He reached his limit this week. We've been talking to him all week long about how to deal with the people in your life who are just not nice and what to do when there's conflict. He hates school, hates India and has a horrible attitude. It's like he's given up. One day, he came home and was so defeated. He asked us very calmly if we would please consider sending him to boarding school. That's when I knew it must be bad. We made boarding school sound awful and it sounded better to him than his current school situation.

On Thursday there was a fun day field trip and he decided he didn't want to go. He didn't want to spend the bus ride and a free-for-all afternoon with the kids who have been harassing him. Friday, there was a disco/end-of-year party. I went to the school to help decorate. When the kids arrived, Connor was the first through the door. Odd, considering I knew he was not looking forward to the event. We went off to the side because he wanted to talk and he begged me to take him home. His teacher gave him grief about the way he'd written a paragraph. She could've just explained what her expectations were. Instead, she said, "Well! Didn't your mother teach you how to write a paragraph? I'm going to have to talk to her!" Bring it on, sister! This is the thing about his teacher, she tears down and criticizes without offering any positive instruction on how to improve. Connor is afraid to ask her for help or to ask any questions. He's afraid to talk to her at all. We're doing as much of the teaching as we can at home. She expects him to know everything already and belittles him when he doesn't know it or could use a simple refresher. Isn't she supposed to *teach*? This kid is so miserable right now. Thankfully, summer is here in 4 days. We'll have two months to build up his confidence and self-esteem again.

Saturday, we attended a fun party which was spread across three houses. There was one house for the kids and dads. It had bouncy castles, catered American kid food and face painting. The second house was set up for the ladies. Manicures, pedicures, jewelry, pashminas and finger food catered by an upscale hotel. It was lovely. The third house was where everyone congregated after the kids went home. Biriyani and other Indian dishes were served. Lighting, tents and chairs were set up in the backyard with a projection screen and music. There were Mehndi artists at the party and I had one of my hands done. Because of the humidity, it took a long time to dry and I managed to smudge it just about everywhere. The palm turned out dark, which I'm told is a good thing, and the back of my hand is very light.

The rest of our weekend was spent unpacking boxes and swimming. Sunday, we went to Sparky's for a late lunch. The restaurant was filled with Americans. It was nice to see familiar faces at lunch. We may go there more regularly on Sundays. The owner was seated with us while we were ordering. When I asked that the white gravy not be put on my chicken, the owner said to the waiter three times, "No gravy on top of the chicken!" It reminded me of an Amelia Bedelia moment. "Amelia, no gravy on top of the chicken!" We laughed so hard when my chicken arrived and there was no gravy on top. Nope, it was underneath. Thank you Amelia Bedelia!

Today, our new housekeeper/cook starts. Can't you just hear my relief as you read this? We're also getting the last of furniture shipment today. More boxes. Ugh!

Rant and Roll

More boxes. More broken furniture. Six missing boxes. More marked up walls. More peeved off.

The language barrier got the best of me combined with an utter lack of respect for our property and belongings. Watch out...she's gonna blow!

I had my rant about furniture specifically marked with arrows that point which end is up and broken crown mouldings when said furniture is upside down. I was met with blank stares. I came upstairs and told The King (who was directing and keeping an eye on our office electronics) to have them bring everything into the living room and please leave.

The King came back upstairs to inform me that the gas grill was too large to bring into the living room. Would it be ok if they put it in the garage? And I was so hoping to grill something in the living room tonight.

Ready for the best part? After I ranted, the supervisor: A) Asked me for a tip. I ranted again. B) Didn't want to sign the paper that stated 6 boxes were missing, as well as the items that had shipped inside the the bookcases. There were big X's cut into the paper, the contents were gone. C) Had the guts to give me a customer survey to fill out. Seriously.

I went to lunch with a friend to distract me from my icky morning. I have been blessed to have made a friend here who listens when I need to rant and sorts me out I need that too. As it turned out, the Rice Krispies treats that I made for her party Saturday night were gross. I don't know if it was because the butter was a yucky brand, or if it was just rancid altogether. I had some of the butter on muffins Sunday morning and commented about how gross it was. I'd forgotten that I'd used it for the Rice Krispie squares the night before. It's a small thing, really, but it was the proverbial straw. What was I to do but console myself with alcohol or dessert. I was at a dry restaurant, and quite frankly, I think I'd rather be fat than a mid-afternoon drunk. Dessert was terrific. A brownie was served over cashews in a hot pan (think sizzling fajitas) and topped with ice cream. When it arrived at the table, the waiter poured chocolate sauce over it. The chocolate sizzled and bubbled. It was a lovely mixture of caramelized chocolate, crunchy cashews, cold ice cream and chewy brownie to take a bite out of a stressful morning.

On the happy side...Connor had a good day at school. Yay!! He had another field trip and since this one was for science, he wasn't getting out of it. There were no major incidents. Thank God for small favors! He had no homework tonight so we're going to go hit the pool. If I don't post tomorrow, it will because I sank to the bottom after the sizzling brownie concoction.

Kramer's First Vet Appt.

I went to the vet the other day with a friend who was bringing her kitties in to have them fixed. I wanted to scope out the vet clinic and meet the vet. I explained to the vet that Kramer has inhalant allergies. He's been treated for this in the past in Illinois. Our new vet, Dr. Mohamed didn't bat an eye about the allergies but insisted that Kramer didn't need heartworm meds in India. That night, I called our vet back home who said he would feel better if we kept Kramer on heartworm and flea meds for his entire stay in India.

The vet's office has a waiting area where there are displays of pet food. Suggestion: check the expiration date before you buy. Off the waiting area there is a sliding door that leads to one small dimly lit room containing reception/billing/examination/surgery. Let me break that down for you. The operation table is in the middle of the room with a computer desk to the left. In the desk is a drawer for all the monetary transactions. The vet handled every aspect of our visit from the time we arrived until the time we left. There were two doors off the multi-purpose room, one appeared to be a kitchen. I'm not sure what the other one was. (I later found out it was a room with an x-ray machine and a staircase.)

I went back in today for our appointment. I got the impression that Dr. Mohamed was not ready to accept that Kramer has allergies. Kramer's symptoms: sneezing, chewing on his back feet, pink weepy eyes, pink swollen tissue around his mouth and sometimes it sounds like he's trying to clear his throat. I'll admit that when the Illinois vet first said that it was allergies, I thought he was nuts. I figured it was a crack-diagnosis to charge me big bucks. The treatment worked within hours. Once Kramer gets a shot of cortisone, he was a different dog. Today, the doc asked all kinds of questions. Is the dog lonely? Is there anything wrong with his feet? Does he get enough exercise? No because he can't spend long periods of time outside because of his *allergies*. I'm sure he's a fine veterinarian. I'm guessing he just doesn't see a lot of people wanting to pay to treat their pets allergies.

I championed for my pooch and Kramer got the shot. He's feeling much better, although thirsty which is normal. He goes back in two weeks for a follow up. Today's treatment cost $3.75. In the US it used to cost about $100.00. How about that?

One more thing about Kramer...he loves mehndi. Every time he comes near me, he licks my henna hand.

What in The World...

...Has happened to my taste buds?

At lunch today, I had a Tomato Caliente Quesadilla. It has tabasco sauce in it. It tasted a bit flat so I piled the pico de gallo on top of it.

Tonight, we ordered veggie pizza which was laden with jalepeno peppers. I ate them and they didn't seem hot to me. I remember the first time I tried a jalepeno, tears ran down my face from the burning.

My tastebuds have adjusted to India before the rest of me. What's up with that?

Good Things Do Happen in India

Here are the good things that have happened today...

- **Last day of school!** Technically, tomorrow is the last day of school but with the report card in hand we're blowing that pop stand!

- Report card day and considering the rough couple of months that Connor had, his grades were very acceptable, all A's and B's. The comment section didn't contain anything unexpected either, which was great. Negativity was curbed and that was a good thing.

- I went to the tailor to pick up a few of my Salwar Kameez sets. I tried them all on and I feel silly wearing them--especially the dupatta (scarf). It will take a little getting used to. The were made exactly to my measurements...a good thing!

- Our new housekeeper/cook, Mani, is (so far) a dreeeeeeeam. She cooks, she cleans, she irons, she shops. I visit, I lunch, I shop, I socialize, I play. Mani was pleased that I was wearing Indian style earrings today and was going to have Indian clothing made. Apparently that meant I wasn't too much of a loser and an invitation was extended to attend her niece's wedding (we'll be away). She just arranged my dupatta for me. Well, first she laughed, then she arranged it. She's insisting I get a saree. Sounds like someone else I know but I'm not naming names (but you know who you are)! Mani is a good thing!

- We've booked a week long trip to the Maldives in June. I was very worried about leaving Kramer with the staff. Usually, our driver would work out of the car rental office when his assigned family is out of town (at half his wage). I asked if he would consider coming to work every day while we're away to look after Kramer. He's trilled to not only get his regular pay, but overtime as well. He was very pleased that I trust him to take care of Kramer. Kramer will be happy because out of all the staff, he spends the most time with McGyver. I don't have to worry about Kramer or the mechanics of life at the ranch with someone I trust keeping an eye on things. It may sound trivial but it's a load off my mind. When I told Mani that she would have the week off with pay, she said it's too boring and she'd like to come to work anyway. Suit yourself, I say. Good staff is a good thing. The Maldives? A veeeery good thing.

- I have a friend in Peoria who might be moving to Asia. In fact, they might even end up in India. I won't say any more about it because I don't want to jinx it. But I will be ecstatic if it happens.

India is becoming more and more of a good thing.

Mayajaal

JB took the afternoon off work to come out and play. After hair cuts for both of them, we ventured to Mayajaal (http://www.mayajaal.com/) to see a movie. This is the place that Connor was supposed to go with his class on a field trip. We decided to see *Pirates of the Caribbean*. We didn't care for it, so we left during the intermission. That was an hour and half into it and I was so relieved! When we paid for the tickets, we were given assigned seats. There were about 10 people in the theater and they were all assigned seats side-by-side in the back row. We broke out and sat in the middle of the room--big rebels.

Before the movie, the guys went on the go-karts. JB is so competitive. Apparently, the three Indian guys that he raced against were too in their various shades of pink shirts, but they were no match for JB. As the race ended, one guy scooted into the parking bay before JB. This guy was so pleased with himself, he said, "Did you see? I overcome you before the end." Uh huh. Oookaaay.

This all takes place at a shopping mall (1 store) with restaurants (Baskin Robbins and movie food) and entertainment (one large screen with Indian music videos).

Since I brought up the Indian music videos, let's venture into that topic for a moment. Scantily clad women (even by American standards) gyrating and rolling around on the floor with their duet partners. It makes me wonder...how is it offensive to wear shorts or a sleeveless top in India? How does Richard Gere playfully kissing an Indian actress warrant a reaction of burning effigies and possible prosecution? I don't have the answers either. It's just "one of those things."

We had a little more time to spare before the movie so we decided to bowl a string. I was wearing flip flops and didn't have socks to wear in the rental shoes, so just the guys were going to bowl. They paid for two players, one string each. In typical Indian fashion, we weren't allowed to press any of the buttons. They set up one person for one string. When I tried to explain that it was for two people, he nodded, pointed and said, "Now he go," referring to Connor. But that means they each bowl half a string, not each one string. And how do you know each person's score if two people are taking turns on one string? Are you all following me on this!? As it turns out, people here just bowl barefoot anyhow, so we bowled three people to one string. There were lanes where five people stood around the lane, barefoot, taking turns on one string (if you're a math wiz, that's two balls each and then they're done). On the board behind the cashier, it said "No Sharing." I just don't get it. JB (AKA Mr. Competitive) is quite a bit more aggressive in bowling than the native folks. His were faster, the crashes louder and the strikes more plentiful. Every time JB had his turn, the crash of pins made everyone stop and look in the awkward silence that followed. When I bowled, everyone looked away. That's what you get for bending over wearing pants, shocked expressions and turned heads. I did not take the opportunity to wear one of my new Salwars...live and learn.

So, here's the bottom line...

3 Movie tickets for *Pirates*: $9

3 Go-Kart tickets for 2 people: $11.25

1 string of bowling for 3 people to share (no shoe rental): $3

2 popcorn and 3 sodas: $4

Drive each way: 1 hour

The "been there, done that" experience of Mayajaal with no repeats: priceless!

The Weekend Lawn Caper

The lawn mower was delivered on Sunday by a toy-like little truck. Both the mower and the delivery truck look like Fisher-Price toys. Maybe that's insulting to Fisher-Price because they make good quality toys and the lawn mower looks like it could fall apart at any time. It has the look of more like a dollar-store find, except it was more expensive than a decent lawn mower would be in the US. It took four men about two hours to get it working properly (somewhat). While they tried to figure it out, blades were changed, a mechanic was called in and the lawn was massacred.

I explained that the container on the back was a must, otherwise Kramer would be dragging grass into the house. The gardener has decided that the grass collecting container creates too much work to empty it every so many passes. Instead, it's been taken off and wads of grass are being swept off the lawn with brooms into large containers and emptied into the trash bin outside the gate. The sweeper is helping him but I don't think she's too impressed about him creating extra work for her.

Yesterday was our first day of summer break. It included the beginning of a five-part series on attitude and some math work. We'll also be working on further developing writing skills in the weeks to come. All afternoons are reserved for fun. McGyver is a creating a touristy list of things for us to do. (Which we never did.) Yesterday, Connor had a playdate. Today, we're going bowling with friends. Tomorrow, he has another playdate. His classmates all added one another to their MSN chat programs, so he's been chatting with them online and getting to know them better. I hope this helps when he goes back to school in the fall. The girl who was harassing him has gone back to her home country. Things are definitely looking up for him.

Another Amelia Bedelia moment in the kitchen. "Please roast a chicken for dinner." Next time, please specify that the chicken should go breast-up--preferably with the head removed--add a little water, onion, spices and cook until the meat longer. I took the legs and breast meat off, cooked it again and disposed off the head and carcass before JB saw it. Otherwise, nobody would've eaten it. It's my own fault. I'm learning that I need to be more specific. When I wasn't specific about the cinnamon rolls last week, they were rolled up, sliced about 3 inches long and baked sideways. They were cinnamon logs! They did taste yummy though.

Money, Money, Money, Monaaay

Money. We currently don't have any and everyone wants some. Let me explain...

I'm missing my favorite solitaire diamond earrings. It's not unlike me to take my earrings off and put them somewhere to not be found for a long period of time. I asked the housekeeper (Mani) if she had noticed them laying around anywhere. She said no and I asked her if she would keep an eye out for them.

(The rest of this story comes later in the day.) As I was leaving the house, Mani asked us to pay her son's school tuition and take a little out of her pay each month to pay it back. "You want to borrow money?" I asked.

"No, noooo madame. You give me 5000 rupees and you take 1000 or 2000 each pay. Like that."

"A loan."

"No, nooo madame...for son's school." It's still a loan, by the way.

Apparently it is common practice to lend money for tuition, some people even pay it on behalf of their staff. At the end of the day 5000 rupees is about $121 US dollars. We've lent more than that to people never to see it be repaid so it didn't seem like a big deal.

The thing is, Mani has worked for us for only one week which makes her request very bold. We said at the beginning that there will be no advancements in pay. We know lots of expats in India who have been burned doing this. Had she worked for us for a year, we might feel differently about it but it's really a practice I don't want to get into. When I want to get out of something, what's my answer? You'll need to talk to Sir about that. Sir was home early last night but she didn't talk to him about it. She probably expects me to ask for her. *head wobble*

We got out the door, albeit running a little late to go bowling. We went to a different venue this time, Snow Bowling--there was no snow though, in case you were wondering about snow in India. We each got to bowl our own games and it was a lot of fun. Connor scored 93 beating everyone, even the grown ups. On our way out, the guys who work at the bowling alley called me over to ask if we enjoyed ourselves. "Yes, we did," I said.

"How about showing your appreciation with a little money?"

"You want money!? You want me to tip you!?" He head wobbled and answered, "Never mind madame." It was the equivalent of "Hey lady, you look dumb, how about giving me some money for no reason I can think of?" You have to give the guy credit for trying.

On to our passport photos. JB couldn't find the batch that we had taken when we first moved here so off we went to Konica (and mine turned out really ugly, by the way). As I'm coming down the stairs, I remember JB making a comment about having his own camera to take photos at work and when he travels (inspired by the *Spiderman/Sony* billboard). You see, he fried my Sony Cybershot and I don't trust him to take good care of my big bad Cannon Rebel. I decided to get him his own camera for Father's Day. When I go to pay for it I realized that when I left the ATM just minutes before, I had left my ATM card in the machine and walked away. In my defense, I was looking at my receipt noticing that the whole card number was printed on it...very dangerous. I was also trying to stuff money into my wallet. Money that is actually too large in size to fit properly in an American-sized wallet. I was distracted and, I admit, I'm a dummy.

When I got home, I was a little cranky. Actually, that's wrong. I was really peeved off with myself. I have quite a track record for doing this stupid kind of stuff. Triple-booking non-refundable flights on different airlines (it was an accident), booking hotel rooms for the night before we arrive at a destination only to find out there's a big convention and there are no rooms available anywhere in town (not one of my finer moments, we had to drive 2.5 hours to go back home). And I'm sure there's more. As soon as I walked through the door, Mani launches into this tirade about me accusing her of taking my diamond earrings. Then she launches into another snit about how McGyver could've taken them (wha??) and why blame her? Apparently something got lost in translation. I explained to her that I wasn't accusing anyone of anything. I misplace my own things all the time (remember, I'm a dumbass!) and I just wanted her to be aware in case she came across them while cleaning. Then I tried to explain to her what happened with the bank card as my way of getting the point across that there is no money (ie: there is no loan). It didn't work. I'm pretty sure she didn't believe me.

At this point, I was very tired of being yelled at and feeling like an idiot. What's a girl to do at this point? Dessert, usually. But I went for a nap instead, joined by Connor and Kramer fighting for JB's side of the bed. We did sort out the ATM card fiasco. New cards will take two weeks to arrive. The bank was very good about expediting them to India when our billing address is still in Illinois. In the meantime, and please don't tell our staff this, we can transfer money into Connor's account over the internet and use his ATM cards...

Apparently, Danie's not quite a dummy after all!

My Soap Opera

When we went out to dinner tonight, I skipped to the loo on my way into the restaurant. Before coming back out again, I stopped to wash my hands. I put my hand bag on the counter and looked to the left for the soap machine, nope that's the paper towel dispenser. I hear a whir-whir-whir-whir sound and when I turn my head to see where the sound is coming from I notice my open handbag has set off the automatic soap dispenser. Sweet-smelling slimy soap was automatically squirting into my bag over and over again. It dripped down the handle and was smeared all over my notebook, wallet and, well, everything.

Good times.

What Do Expats Miss?

Family, friends and food. Depending on the day, perhaps not in that order.

I have been surfing Top Secret Recipes (http://www.topsecretrecipes.com) all morning. A couple of our favorite restaurants are listed and many of my lunch time meet-the-girls hot spots have recipes available for printing.

I'm hungry.

When it Rains, it Pours

It is chucking it down right now! It's the first time I've seen rain since we've lived here. Thunder, lightening and beaucoup water falling from the sky.

It's a beautiful thing!

Facebook

A friend sent me a link to http://www.facebook.com. The rest is history. I was falling asleep at the keyboard while I was still on this website. I went to bed and got up again to do one more search, even more slumped over the keyboard. I've been catching up with people I have seen in nearly 20 years. Gasp! I'm old enough to not have seen people in 20 years! Despite that depressing thought, Facebook has been a blast. You've been warned. Go there at your own risk. But go anyway. And when you do, check out the group that I've created for Expats in India.

Miss Communication

I thought I exhibited extraordinary patience with no phone service for 5 days, but when the internet service had been cut yesterday, I nearly went out of my mind! By this morning, I had the sweats and the shakes. No news, no stock updates, no email, no shopping, no recipes and no Facebook.

You can't stick a girl in India with no way of communicating with the outside world. Not unless there's a huge amount of dessert or drugs available. Forget I said that, I'd take the internet over dessert any day of the week. The internet is my crack.

People have been relocating to and living in other countries all around the world for many years. How on earth did they survive before the internet? Communicating with family took weeks, if not months, by letter. Communicating by phone would have been very expensive and inconsistent, it certainly wouldn't have involved live cameras. Researching the relocation destination came from what little outdated information that could be found in an encyclopedia. There would be no meeting people 'virtually' in advance. No internet shopping to have your homeland comforts shipped to you in record time.

So, Phone Guy showed up today. The internet was finally back on, but still no phone. He came in, disconnected the modem, plugged the phone and declared, "No problem madame." The King explained to him that the telephones had no dial tone. Phone Guy had to call his supervisor to get permission to fix the phone line. Only Supervisor Guy said, "No problem," as well. Funny how we had no problem with our phone service up until this past Friday but it's not the phone company's problem. There was only one exchange of looks that said, 'Not my problem,' and 'You're not getting through this door until it's fixed,' and we were back in business. I'm getting better with communicating via facial expression...no language barrier there.

From miscommunication to Miss Communication. I'm back online!

The Boss

There's been a buzz in Chennai all week about a movie that hits theaters today. Four days ago, I was told that *Sivaji-The Boss* is completely sold out in Chennai for the first 20 days that it will be showing.

'The Boss' actor, Rajinikanth, is from Bangalore. H is adored by southern Indian movie-lovers. There are huge billboards all over the city promoting this movie and the products that he endorses. In newspapers, next to pictures of 'Brangelina' you'll find The Boss...he's that big here.

There's another Boss in the news today, India may get their first female President: Pratibha Patil. I wonder if the US will follow suit.

Adoption, Still Not an Option

Happy Father's Day to all dads and step dads out there!

As personal as this is, I'm putting it right out there with the hope that somebody somewhere will read this and tell me how wrong I am.

We've been trying to adopt a child for four years and have continually had doors close on us. This is something we knew we wanted to do since we were 19 years old. It was always part of our plan to have a child on our own and then fill the house with adopted children. Just when we meet a British lady in the Bahamas who tells us it can be done (she did it), we get our hopes only to be told no again. Just when we decide we're not going to take no for an answer and will hire as many attorneys as necessary, we get moved to India. Upon moving to India, a country that has 12.4 million orphans, we thought this was God's way of opening a door for us. Instead, it's been one more disappointing door closed to adoption.

We are Canadian citizens. Surely, we are not the first and only Canadian citizens living outside of Canada who have wanted to adopt. Surely, it's been done before! If it hasn't, how broken is that system?

We couldn't adopt while living in the US because we weren't US citizens. It sounds ridiculous, I know. Yet, we can't adopt through Canada, because we don't live there. In India, there are only about 5000 adoptions per year and they happen through Delhi. A person can be awarded 'guardianship' here but not become adoptive parents until the child is taken back to your own country for the adoption process. That process, again, doesn't work unless you're definitively moving back to your home country.

There are three solutions to this that we know of:

1) Private adoption of a newborn while we live in the US.

2) Become US citizens. Or,

3) Move back to Canada.

...None of which are feasible solutions to us for a variety of reasons. There has got to be another solution.

What happens when your home country isn't your home anymore? Too darn bad for you and for the children who could have parents? I just can't believe that.

Email us and tell us how wrong we are. Please.

danie@earthtodanie.com

Back to School

Summer is over and school is back in session...for Indian kids. The company built a school on the factory property in the early 90's but not much has been done there since. Apparently no MD has ever gone to visit the school so they were taken back when JB paid them a visit. As he toured the school, each class stood up to greet him.

They were asked to provide a list of what they need. Among the list, more water faucets in the bathroom (there's one bathroom with one water faucet for the whole school), some classrooms don't have desks and the children sit on the floor, more classrooms are needed, and they need a bus so they can provide transportation to students (ensuring they get an education). Additional items needed are playground equipment, computers and science equipment.

Before JB toured the school, we had discussed ways of volunteering and supporting the school. When he talked to the Head Mistress about it, she seemed delighted but had never had volunteers. She wasn't sure what we could do. JB suggested we could do whatever they needed us to do, anything from reading to the kids to painting walls. OK, the painting-thing didn't go over so well. He was met with a blank look...I don't think they're down with the idea of the MD's wife doing the painting. We figure a company-wide work day might be more acceptable to her.

It's my hope that we can do some good here. The company, as well as, our family.

The Maldives: Diving Into Vacation

We went on ☐
in the Indian Ocean. I took lots of photos with an underwater disposable camera, I hope some turn out nicely. We saw a Manta Ray. JB and Connor saw a ☐
always in awe of God's creativity and His generosity to us. He created a wonder like that for us to enjoy. Truly inspiring.

Another thing we☐
dish Connor☐
at a Teppenyaki. I'll probably have to lock up all the knives when we get back home. He thought of it as Ninja Cooking. His eyes were far too wide and he enjoyed it far too much! The beef was Australian. Connor suggested to the chef that he just bring the whole cow to our table.

Today's itinerary includes lots of boredom and maybe a spa treatment. We're having a private dinner on the beach tonight. We checked the menu last night...seafood and steaks. Perhaps I should call ahead and ask them to bring Connor the entire cow. He'd like to know why vegetables couldn't be sacred in India...then he wouldn't have to eat them.

There are t-shirts in the boutique that say, "Maldives: The Art of Doing Nothing." Love it!

Home Sweet Home

Happy Canada Day! We'll be spending Canada Day unpacking and running a few errands to get ready for the week.

We got home last night from the Maldives. As the boat pulled away from Kurumba, I was so sad! I was anticipated some re-entry culture shock and I was just so sad to leave paradise. All in all, our flights went smoothly considering the flooding in Mumbai and the number of flights being rerouted. We had a few canceled, rescheduled, and delayed flights but it was all handled very efficiently until we arrived in Trivandrum. They gave our seats away and weren't going to let us board. Luckily, we had lots of help on our return journey as well and they helped to get us on the flight. Actually, they held the flight while they discussed and rediscussed what they would do. We got on the flight, although none of our seats were together. Arriving in Chennai, the jetway was installed at the door on the left side of the plane. We were disembarked on the right side of the plane and stood out on the tarmac to wait for busses. I won't even comment on JB's rant about all of all this. Me? I just chalk it up to "that's traveling."

We had a lovely welcoming committee in Chennai. Both drivers, the travel agent, an airport representative and millions of mosquitoes. The agent and the rep were apologizing profusely about the mix up on our last flight. They wanted to be assured that we would use their services again. I just stood off to the side, eavesdropping with my eyeballs involuntarily rolling back in my head.

We went home with McGyver while JB's driver waited for our luggage. They brought it to the house about an hour later. Again, I love not having to schlep the bags. Three years from now, we'll move somewhere else and I'm going to be spoiled, spoiled, spoiled.

On the drive home, here's what I realized...I had actually missed India. While I would never encourage someone to travel back to their homeland in the early days of an expat assignment, I think a trip anywhere else is a great idea. Coming back to India was coming home. We missed our stinkin' mutt and it was heaven to sleep in our own beds. Mani came in on Friday and baked some cinnamon rolls for us. The horns were honking, the staff were squabbling and, oh right, two green snakes fell from a tree (not sure yet what kind they were, non-venomous I'm told) McGyver shot video with his mobile phone...of course he did. So, all is right in the our world.

Back To Reality

As we sink back into reality, and hey, I'm not complaining because it's a decent reality to sink into, I can't help but long for a vacation. It's raining Green Tree Pit Vypers[1] and Cobras out there. The worst of it in the Maldives were geckos and the Fruit Bat[2]. JB had his shoes on for about 10 minutes before a baby Gecko[3] began wiggling around in the toe of the shoe. I'd have freaked out and screamed like a girl. Well, that's pretty much what he did too and I can't blame him for it! The Fruit Bats are also known as Flying Foxes. They are massive. In fact, when you watch a scary movie with the creepy, massive bats--these are it. They're of no threat to humans and they're not nocturnal but when you see one of those babies flying above your head, you can't help but get creeped out. Creepy, I admit. But neither were dangerous, so not so bad, right?

Here's my other reality, and I hate the question, "What's for dinner?" I hated it in the US and I hate even more in India. "Tonight," I told them, "is Olive Garden." Mani isn't impressed with the menu but I haven't sunk into my Indian food reality yet, so just let me wallow in food denial, ok?

[1] http://en.wikipedia.org/wiki/Trimeresurus

[2] http://en.wikipedia.org/wiki/Fruit_bat

[3] http://en.wikipedia.org/wiki/House_Gecko

Dupatta

Kameez

Punjabi Pant

Salwar Kameez

I had my first corporate wife gig last night. It was dinner with an out-of-town business associate in which Connor and I were both expected to attend. He did great! It started at 8:30pm so it ended quite late.

We had reservations at a very traditional Indian restaurant. Silver cups, small silver bowls and banana leaves lined the silver trays. I liked it. I may go silver shopping! If you come to dinner when we move back to the US, don't expect the banana leaf lining, that's a southern India thing. We ate with our fingers but occasionally I did have to cut or scoop something with a spoon. We just went with whatever our hostess ordered for us so I was a little nervous. Everything tasted wonderful. It was not too spicy and it was a nice variety.

This is the first time that I've worn a full-on Salwar Kameez. Let me just say, these are not the most flattering outfits. They're meant to be comfortable and to hide all womanly features--tents, basically. My goal here was to be respectful without being ridiculous. Frankly, I felt ridiculous. I'm not so good with dupattas. I half strangle myself with them when I get in the car, get it caught in doors or have one end dragging on the ground. Looking at the photo, I think I was wearing the dupatta a little too high. I'm working on it though.

Jewelry was kept simple, my normal American stuff with the exception of ankle bracelets. They're worn on both ankles and have a few bells. Yes, they jingle when I walk. Connor says he can even hear them below water in the pool when we're swimming. I have plain silver anklets with one set of bells but these things can get very thick and very ornate.

The lady that we had dinner with made a comment on my outfit which made me wonder if it was a compliment or a back-handed insult. I'm still not sure. I told her that I only dress like this for special occasions or to have dinner with someone special such as herself. She seemed pleased with that.

Pranks and Geckos

Don't read this if you're expecting deep insights on culture, politics or religion in India. Oh no. I'm far too shallow and lack the intelligence necessary for that. I'm not an expert about anything. I'm just here for a good time and amusing myself about it to stay sane.

So, with that said, let me start this story by telling you about my cheeky son. At the risk of beating a dead horse, this story is actually about another gecko but it starts with Mr. Cheeky...

Over the past week, while I was in my post-vacation cranky stupor, Connor was moving things around the house. I have no idea where he got the notion to start this prank, but it was driving me nuts. Half way through the week, I was complaining to my husband at the dinner table about our housekeeper. She does a great job dusting but doesn't put anything back in its rightful place. All week long I was going behind her moving things back to where they belong. Books lying in front of the bookends, table clocks turned backwards, photo frames moved around and so on. Connor nearly spit out his pasta with laughter, "That's not Mani, that's *me*!" We all laughed over the long list of items he pranked me on. Connor promised he would stop, but he didn't. So when I saw his Gameboy laying around, I thought I'd move it. He's 10 so it had to be a big move for him to notice. Ok, I hid it. This morning he wanted it back but I told him I would have to get it for him because I couldn't reveal such a good hiding place. With his usual impatience, he went off to see if he could find it.

Off he went to search for his Gameboy--evil-laughing all the way downstairs. He had something up his sleeve. He was going to move something else! He came back upstairs and said he had a present for me, then he shoved this in my face...

He was going to hide a lint roller. Or as we call it, a Kramer remover. A nosy gecko walked onto it, got stuck and couldn't get himself off. Connor pronounced him DOA. And yeah, I screamed like a wimpy girl in a horror flick.

I have to pause here to say that "Kramer removers" are an imported item, therefore I wasn't about to waste an entire roll because of one dead gecko. With a shedding golden retriever, we go through these things very quickly.

I was feeling very brave since the gecko was dead and I began to peel the layer of sticky paper. That's when *he moved*. Remember the movie *Scream*? I could've easily have had the lead role. The gecko wasn't dead, he was just stuck and neither one of us were about to rescue his poor little reptile soul. We couldn't even call on McGyver since he's away (and we dismissed the relief driver on Sunday). King George took care of it for us.

If you'd like the "he said, she said" of this story. Check out Connor's blog for his version.

http://heheelys.blogspot.com/2007/07/dead-or-alive.html

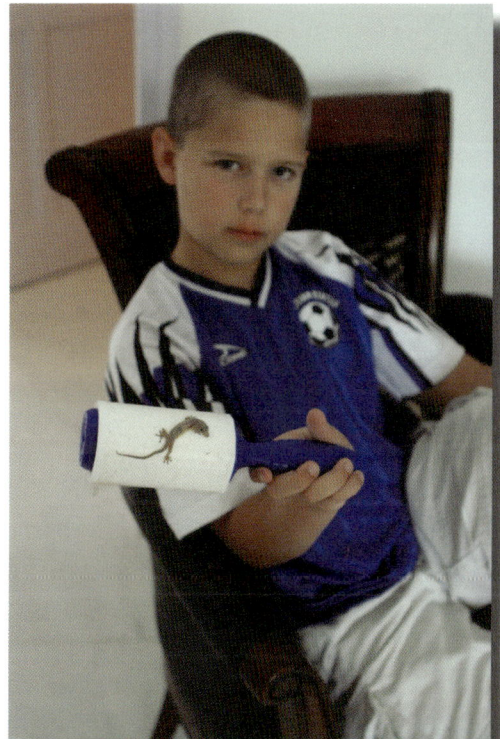

Ruined Pants, Ruined Shoes.

There are days when India is very frustrating. Today was such a day.

I was really excited when I went to the tailor several weeks ago to pick up my new Salwar Kameez sets. My favorite set was one that had white pants with pretty blue embroidery and pleats down the sides of both pant legs. I was very disappointed when I put on the pants and they didn't fit. All the other pieces fit perfectly.

It's not like popping into a store to return or exchange an item of clothing. This process is much more involved. I went back to the tailor with pants in hand and explained they didn't fit at all. He re-measured me and re-measured the pants, and looked at me like it was my fault, not his. If it were my fault, I would've brought back *all* the pairs of pants. He said he could fix them by using a different white material for the part around the hips but it wouldn't necessarily match. I figured that would be fine because it would be covered by the kameez anyhow.

He told me the date the pants would be ready. I gave an extra week before I went to pick them up...they're weren't ready. He told me, "Monday." I gave an additional few days and went back today (Thursday). The tailor had them ready and was folding them as I walked in. He showed me the top of the pant, which looked fine but that's all I saw before he folded and bagged them. I thanked him for fixing his mistake and then he told me about the extra charge! I paid it, but I wasn't happy about it.

When I got home, I tried on the pants. The pretty blue embroidery and pleats are now down the front of the pant leg. It looks ridiculous. Picture your Adidas sweat pants with the stripe down the front of your thighs. Picture a police officer with the stripe down the front of his leg. Silly! I just paid extra money for a pair of pants that I can't wear. It was my very favorite pair too. Bummer.

I know you're reading this and probably thinking, what's the big deal? The big deal is the sleazy way the whole transaction was handled, my disappointment and the fact that there's really no recourse now. I'm angry at myself for letting down my how-can-I-be-ripped-off-today guard. Perhaps on any other day, it might not have been a big deal at all. But today, it's a little vignette of how frustrating life can be in India.

Yesterday, King George informed me that the housekeeper should keep her shoes inside the house because Kramer got a hold of them and the King had to chase him around the yard to get them back. Today was the first day that Mani put her shoes inside the door. When we got home from the tailor, Kramer had eaten one of Mani's shoes. We paid for her ruined shoes and had McGyver drive her home in her bare feet.

I feel the need for a shopping outing. Maybe in the US.

Maybe soon.

The Honeymoon Is Over

In the life of every expat, a little angst must fall. What I'm going through right now is very normal and even expected. I've hit the 4 to 6 month period where the honeymoon is over and everything is making me angry. Thankfully, I know this is just a phase but it does take some time to get through it. Overall, I'm still quite happy and I don't regret our decision to move here. But the frustrating moments are more frequent and more intensified. This too shall pass...this too shall pass...this too shall pass...

It is necessary for us to adjust to life in India, however odd it may be to us at times, or however offensive, even. It is not for India to adjust to us...that's what I keep telling Connor. At the age of ten, it's all about what's fair. We encounter situations on a daily basis where the values and manners we are teaching him are contradicted by the way we're treated. It offends his sense of fairness. And well, it offends me too.

Yesterday, on our way into the mall, there was a man sitting on the sidewalk wearing a short lungi. Essentially, it's a piece of fabric tied in such a way that it looks like a mini skirt. Lungi Guy was sitting with his knees up and jockeying for a more comfortable position. Unfortunately for anyone in the near vicinity, an eyeful was had of everything that was under the lungi. I don't want to see that! I don't want to see people urinating in the street or hanging their butts over the side of a bridge like it's their personal toilet, either. And since I'm on a roll...I don't want to see the amount of trash that there is in the streets. It's just getting to me.

Once at the mall, our mission was to see the Harry Potter movie. We teach our children to be polite, to wait their turn, to be considerate of other people. While we were standing in line to be let into the theater we experienced the usual stuff...shoving, cutting in line etc. I don't want to make waves here so I didn't say anything. Occasionally, when JB gets shoved, he'll say, "Excuse me," rather loudly. It's not like that accomplishes anything. My theory is that the seats are assigned, so I don't see any benefit to shoving us aside to get inside first. I'm actually ok with being shoved and being pushed farther and farther back in line, but when someone shoves my child aside or cuts in line in between us, it makes me a little crazy around the edges. Everyone knows, even rude people, that you do not separate a parent from their child. Unless you're in India, that is. Then it's every man for himself and to heck with the little kid who's in the way.

The movie was very good. Ever since we lived in England, Connor has been a big Harry Potter fan. Movies are such a nice distraction. They temporarily let us forget where we are, especially when it's been a rough day. The problem is that it's like a vacation and you know how I am when I come back to reality...eek! When we left the theater, more shoving and pushing, and screw your kid. We were getting a lot of odd looks and it took us a while to figure out that it was because we were carrying our movie-trash. In a country where its acceptable to dump your trash absolutely anywhere, why would the movie theater be any different? There were no bins to be found in the theater area. It wasn't until we got out to the mall that we finally found a bin and threw away our rubbish.

That became my fifth or sixth "cultural moment" of the day. It can be exhausting.

Movies have become an important outlet for us. We ordered a DVD projector from the US and had it shipped by courier to JB's office...not a cheap endeavor. We've been enjoying projecting movies, video games and iPod TV onto the wall of our family room. Friends of ours have the previous model of this projector and they were able to make it region-free with a software patch. Great idea if you're always moving around the world, then it doesn't matter where you buy DVDs. Our projector only played US DVDs, so we decided to try the same software patch. Is our projector region-free? No, it's completely busted and needs to be sent back to the US to be repaired. Considering the cost to repair it plus the shipping costs, it was the same price and faster to just buy a new one.

This week, we will be celebrating 15 years of marriage. Now there's a honeymoon that is definitely not over.

Amen.

14 Snakes in 4 Months

The King has been keeping track of the snakes. Today, he informed me that we've had 14 snakes since we've lived here.

Two of those 14 were today. The first one was a Green Vine Snake. The guards took care of it without any problems. Five minutes later, another snake fell from the same tree, it was a Rat Snake. The guard went after it, but it was very fast. It went down the driveway to the back yard. It slithered it's way into the servant quarters and into the toilet. After two hours of messing around with the snake, the guards called me on the intercom to use my cell phone so they could call Snake Guy. When I went out, the snake was in the sewage pipe. They were trying to flush it out. The concern was that the snake would enter the pipes leading into the house and find its way into one of our bathrooms. Can you imagine would that would be like?

The Rat Snake poked his out of the toilet and decided it's not such a good time to come out. It went back into the pipe. Note the Indian style toilet. I'm thinking high-chair toilets are the way to go.

Now everyone is in on the action, two security guards, the gardener, the relief driver and the housekeeper/cook. She liked the idea of emptying a whole imported can of Comet down the toilet. This is the "poison 'im out" technique. Apparently, this technique had been previously implemented with some other substance and had failed. This was a cunning snake and he wasn't surrendering yet.

The "burn 'im out" technique was tried, but thankfully, Snake Guy arrived! After he moved on to the "boil 'im out" technique (which was also unsuccessful...this involved pouring boiling water down the drain while the other end was plugged), he opted for the "drown 'im out" method. They brought in the hose and completely filled the pipe with water so the snake would have no choice but to come out.

Four hours later--here it is--and it was a big sucker too.

Connor and McGyver are both sick with the flu, so they missed the whole thing. Connor slept through it all. JB arrived home just before Snake Guy left with his bag of treasure, so he got to see it up close and personal. JB can't wait to rib McGyver about the number of snakes we've been getting. The poor guy thinks it's a bad sign and that it has something to do with his upcoming marriage. Kramer barked the whole time. He wasn't impressed that he had to stay indoors. Just another day in the life, folks!

Trashy Photos

Since our landlord didn't care enough to do it, we've contracted a company to clean up the garbage outside our gate, restore the curbs and maintain the area. It's embarrassing to live in a nice neighborhood and have so much trash being dumped at our front door.

Here are a few "before" photos. The dumpsters were emptied that morning so it was actually cleaner than usual. Normally, it's piled up 3' high out there, spilling out of the dumpster and most of the time, people don't even bother with the dumpster at all.

While these are not atypical of Chennai, it is atypical for my neighborhood. In fact, there are lots of places in the city that are much worse than this. Every time I see this sight though, I can't help but think, we left "Golf Club" in Illinois for "Trash Club" in India.

The bins have been moved down the street, the curb work has begun and discussions have been had about what will be planted. A suggestion was made that we put some netting on our gate because Kramer has cut his head on it. Netting wasn't available so they've installed metal sheets, making the gate completely solid. At the moment, it's very ugly but I'm hoping that once its painted it won't be so bad. Kramer is barking like a mad dog every time he goes out because he can hear people (and dogs) on the other side of the gate but can't see them. He's afraid. And it worries me when people come into the yard without him seeing them coming.

Signs have been posted (in Tamil and in English) asking people to not dump trash outside our gate and to take it down the street to the new bin location. Unfortunately, people have decided since there's no bin, they'll just dump it into the empty lot. So my fear is that the trash situation (and the snake situation) is going to be worse, not better.

This is the empty lot next door. This is where all the snakes have been coming from.

The landlords came by on the weekend (again) and attempted to gain access to the interior of the house (again) without us being present. I'm glad our day guards have been standing their ground. Apparently, the landlord likes what we were doing to the property and wants to hire the same company to do work at their other property. In the meantime, they made plenty of suggestions to the workers about what they would like done here. I don't think so. If we're paying for improvements to their property, it's going to be done our way. And I'm just about done paying for improvements to this property. The King was very adamant that our work be completed before they go running over to the landlords property. Go George!

Wrap all of that up with a couple of frustrating shopping experiences lately and I'm weary. I'm really looking forward to my sister visiting.

I'm looking forward to getting back to the routine of school. This summer has been a long one staying in Chennai while friends are on home leave. We knew that was going to be the case but it may have been harder than I thought it was going to be. It's nice that everyone is starting to trickle back into town. These are the people that become family when living so far away from relatives.

Apparently, one of our six missing boxes from the move (or the stolen goods from the bookcases) contained retired Longaberger curtains.

With one week to go until my sister arrives for a visit, we needed to get our guest bedrooms sorted out. We went to buy some curtains for her bedroom. We were very pleased when, at the first store we went to, we found plain, tab-top curtains, sans Indian designs that actually would match our two guest rooms. Woo hoo, one stop shopping! Naturally, we were followed around the curtain department by no less than three people eagerly awaiting to help, or to make sure we weren't thieves--I'm not sure which.

We began looking through the stock on the shelves to find the right color and size. We were sort of shoved away and the sales girl took over. We told her we needed 8 panels of blue and 4 panels of green. Up to that point, we had found two panels of blue. She offered to sell us the one on display, like that was the solution to all our problems in life. "But I'll still need 5 more," I said. I was informed that they didn't have them. "OK, what about the green?" No. None. "Can I order them?" Blank stare. The manager comes over and I repeat all my questions again, getting all the same answers. Of course, they don't have them in stock and of course I can't order them, *but* I can buy the single panel on display!

At this point, I should have shut my mouth and walked away. But no, there was a burning question on my brain. One that I knew would defy all logic before I even asked it, but just had to ask it anyway. "Why do you have these panels on display if you don't have any available to sell and they can't be ordered?" There are just no answers to questions this profound. Seriously.

So, we went to another store, and compromising on color and style, we bought the number of panels we needed for three rooms. While hanging all these panels, we realized that perhaps we didn't need quite as many as we thought we would. For three rooms, we had an excess of 3 panels. That's right folks, that meant we were going to have to return them. I know you're probably thinking of zipping into Wal-Mart or Target and returning merchandise while your husband keeps the car running at the curb. You already think that returning merchandise in Canada or the US is painful. You don't know painful. JB suggested I take care of it sometime during the week. I just knew returning something to the store was going to be something I likely don't have the patience for (and I was right). So I wiggled out of it, saying, "Chances are, I won't be able to return the curtains since they were paid for with your credit card." This was our little battle of wills. He didn't want to have to endure it, and I wasn't going to endure it alone.

Yesterday, while I was napping, JB and Connor went to return the panels. They also needed to buy several more in a different color and size for Connor's room. A kid can't wait forever for PB Teen to get the right ones back in stock and have them shipped across the world, you know. When they arrived at the store, they were told to check their bags at the door. How can the curtains be returned if they can't be brought into the store? The security guard read each sku number off of each package and tried to find it on the receipt (there were 22 lines of merchandise on the receipt, so this took a while). Meanwhile, people were waiting at the door with their stuff to be checked and were growing impatient.

They went to the returns desk and waited in line. Again, waiting in line here is like nothing you know until you experience it for yourself. When they got to the desk, they had to wait for someone to come from the curtain department (three floors up) to approve the return. Meanwhile, people were waiting behind them, growing impatient. "What's wrong with the curtains?" The clerk asked.

"Nothing is wrong, I just bought too many and would like to return the ones I don't need."

"You can't return them if there's nothing wrong with them." I'm not sure how the rest of the conversation went, but JB says it took a long time and a lot of discussion before they finally *head wobbled* and relented.

Ok, with his credit in hand, he either needed to stand in line again at the check out to get cash for the credit, or buy something and use the credit toward his purchase. Off they went to gets curtains for Connor. Then they stood in line to purchase them. There was a whole other thing once they got to the check out and the credit needed to be approved blah blah blah. It went on and on. JB said that even the Indian customers were getting peeved off with this whole run around.

On the way home, they stopped by Cafe Coffee Day, the closest thing to a Starbucks in India. We go there regularly and we always order the same thing...Tropical Icebergs. For my fellow Starbucks addicts, these are like mocha frappaccinos. JB ordered two Tropical Icebergs, as he usually does, and this time he was told that they don't serve Tropical Icebergs on the weekend. They only serve another drink which is similar. JB asks what the difference is. "It's basically the same drink, only this one has whip cream and chocolate sauce on top." Seriously. There are times when it's all we can do not to just bang our heads on counters. "I'd like to order two of those drinks that you just described. Please hold the whip cream and chocolate sauce." Imagine that.

Sometimes, that Tropical Iceberg is the highlight of my weekend.

Raindrops Keep Falling On My Head

It's has been unseasonably wet in Chennai. Monsoon season isn't until late in the year but we seem to be getting the leftover bad weather from the South-West Monsoon.

On our way back from dinner recently, it began to rain. Every where we looked, motorcyclists had plastic bags on their heads to cover their hair.

I'm going to take a little hair detour here......

I have to admit, the Indian masses have terrific hair. Not many men seem to have receding hairlines or baldness. Sometimes we'll be stopped at a red light in traffic and I think someone is trying to look into our vehicle. No, they're just checking out their hair. Stop at a red light and watch the combs come flying out of the pockets. JB's driver doesn't want to wear a helmet because it messes up his hair. I can't think of a better nickname for him than "Elvis."

Ok, moving on.......Here's Pool Guy in the rain yesterday. A pool guy who doesn't like to get wet. He was sporting a ball cap, which he doesn't normally wear, and he was trying to maneuver his umbrella so he didn't have to use his hands to hold it. Pool cleaning definitely requires two hands. Three, if it's raining.

Along with the wet weather we've been having, we have various air conditioners and windows around the house that leak. A *lot*. We've been getting puddles in our bedroom when it storms. We've had the AC peeps out here at least four times. Nobody seems to think rain in the house is a big deal. Silly spoiled "Americans" who insist on dry living quarters. Hmph.

I'm not looking forward to Winter Monsoon.

Back to Business

Connor: It's back to school this week and already middle school is shaping up to kick 5th grade's butt. Connor's schedule is already being juggled on a daily basis. Middle schoolers have mandatory band so he had drum orientation this week, meaning early mornings and long days. Connor has also decided to try out for the swim team. Yesterday, he did 60 laps, 1500 meters. He was exhausted last night but excited. The practice requirement is 2 hours, four times per week, either before or after school. So far, he's the only boy in his age range so he's automatically placed on the travel team. I see a trip to Sri Lanka in our near future.

My sister: How much fun am I having with my sister? It's not like we're doing anything special but it's wonderful to have her here. At first, she was overwhelmed with traffic and sights, but yesterday she said she thought she could get used to it. Isn't it always easier for visitors?

Kramer: We had a 911 visit to the vet yesterday with Kramer. Last week, he ate half of an orange flip-flop. Yesterday he began vomiting. We took him to the vet and they did x-rays, barium, and more x-rays. Kramer has 5 or 6 partial blockages that we're hoping will move with laxatives. Kramer is a big pain in the butt when it's time for breakfast or dinner--imagine 24 hours with no food--he's a nightmare. Back to the vet again today for more x-rays. We're praying he won't need surgery.

Culture Shock and Blog Comments

There is a cycle to Culture Shock. Not everyone experiences it but I most certainly do. Every. Single. Time. Even moving from Canada to the US. Even moving from one US state to another US state. I do culture shock. I may be experienced at moving but culture shock isn't something I can control, I just have to go through it. It's kind of like the stages of grief. You have to go through it step by step. You know the next step is coming but you can't control it or back out of it. It's going to happen the way it's meant to happen. Looking back, I've probably spent at least 5 of my last 10 years in some phase of culture shock. I know what it is and I know I have to go through it. I have confidence that I'll go through it in my own way and come out on the other end just fine.

I have found that most expats don't really talk about culture shock. But we all look at one another and know we're each going through it at some level. Some people will say they're fine when they're really not. And then there's me. Let's just put it under a microscope, magnify the details and blog about it! That's all this blog really is, a magnification of the details.

Here are the phases of culture shock:
http://www.doctortravel.ca/tips/culture_shock/

I thought I was somewhere between step 2 and step 3, however I now believe my culture shock is a mesh of both these phases. While things have really been getting on my nerves lately, I can easily laugh about most of the "I can't believe it" kind of stuff. The difference between me and most other people is that I say the stuff most people think but don't say aloud.

Yesterday, this blog had 343 hits from all over the world. I certainly welcome every one to read what I write, that's why I put it out there. I welcome your comments, it's the first thing Connor and I check every morning. I like the feedback and enjoy hearing from family, friends and new friends. If you've never met me and you feel the need to give me unsolicited advice or to make a judgement on my life, please keep in mind that you may think you know me from reading my online journal but you only know what I choose to make public. And that, is not all of me. If you're an Indian citizen living a cushy life abroad, no offense, but I feel you have no place to comment at all on how I'm coping with giving up my cushy life in the US for the one I'm struggling to put together in India.

I know my family is worrying about us. India is so foreign and so unknown to them. I'm sorry that you are watching me go through my deal-with-India phase. You've never heard the behind-the-scenes details of any of our other moves. Believe it or not, it's pretty much the same pattern, maybe just a little more intense this time. Sometimes India makes me laugh and sometimes it makes it cry. I'm OK with that. Please be OK with it too. Staying behind in the US and letting JB work in India was never an option--our family stays together. I'm coming to grips with what it will take for me to make the next three years in India a successful assignment. Failure is not an option, folks. I'm in it for three years. I'll conquer my fears and I'm sure when I leave here I'll be glad I did it. That doesn't mean there won't be struggles along the way and it doesn't mean I'm not going to post about those struggles along with the triumphs.

Truly, we are all doing just fine. I promise.

Harry Potter

Ever since we lived in England where our train station into London was King's Cross--with signs for Platform 9 3/4, a special parking area for brooms, and a place where no muggles were permitted--Connor has been in mad love with the Harry Potter story.

After seeing *The Order of the Phoenix* last week and in anticipation of the last book in the series, he re-read 5 of the 6 novels this week while he was sick. It was all leading up to today, the release of the final Harry Potter book.

I told McGyver yesterday that he may need to come in early today because the books were starting to be sold at 5:30am. I didn't think JB and Connor would go quite that early but I knew that they would be up and ready earlier than usual. McGyver offered to go stand in line and get the book for us. I'm sure he's expecting a huge tip for this service, which we will gladly give him. So here's how it went...

McGyver got up at 2am to stand in line at the book store. He was 10th in line and says there were about 400 people waiting. Now, I know you're likely envisioning this as an orderly group of Americans waiting their turn in line. You're so delusional. Picture 400 people shoving, cutting each other in line and standing on top of you for three and half hours. Seriously, I wouldn't have the heart for it. McGyver must be one tough nut to have stayed 10th in line.

I woke up at my usual 6:30am this morning. I had just sat down at my computer when I heard the gate open. Two minutes later, Connor pulled on some clothes and went running down to greet McGyver with a bag of Mani's treats in hand. He was handed a bag which contained the book, free calendar, Harry Potter Uno and a notice for a Harry Potter musical performed locally. I can only imagine Harry Potter turned into a musical, sung by Indians.

I may have to go for the shock value...that's if I didn't have to endure standing in line.

Credit Where Credit Is Due

I have to give credit to collection agencies. I can't imagine getting ready for work in the morning and thinking, 'Yippee, I get to be a creep again today!'

Connor sprained his wrist during our last week in Illinois. Apparently there was some leftover bill from the doctor visit or x-ray after the insurance company did their thing. I received a call from a collection agency last week telling me we owe a small balance and it's gone to collection. I explained that we had moved to India right after the twisted-arm incident. Our mail isn't guaranteed to arrive here and we hadn't received a bill yet. If she could just send us a bill, we'd be happy to pay it.

I gave her our address and she said she couldn't mail a statement to India. Sure you can! Just stick an extra stamp on it and mail it out. No, statements are sent automatically from a central location, blah blah blah. But did we have the address of a family member to mail the statement to them? Well, sure we do, but we're Canadian and she said they couldn't mail a statement internationally. And no, we don't have a fax machine. JB was at a business dinner and I didn't know his fax number at work.

She said if I could just give her my credit card number, she would just run my card through and we'd be done. *What?* As if I would give my credit card over the phone to someone when I don't even know they are who they say they are. I've had my credit card number stolen before, it's a pain to clean up. Then she asks me to mail her a check. Obviously, somebody isn't wearing their listening hat.

At this point, I'm getting frustrated at answering the same questions over and over again. Why must people be treated like criminals? I told her I was through talking to her about it and if she'd like to talk to my husband, he could call her when he got home. The whole "speak to sir" routine doesn't work so well with Americans. She gave me a 1-800-number. I told her we would need a telephone number with an area code, we can't dial toll free numbers to the US from India. Now she's frustrated and lectures me about the hit our credit rating will take in 30 days. I told her it's really not my problem that she can't find a way to get me a statement. I didn't move to India to run away from a $200 medical bill, but I won't be paying anything without a statement.

As it turns out, the statement was opened by our international banking officer and was paid automatically. We don't owe a dime. Yet, this morning, I received a voice mail from the same person at the collection agency asking us to call her back immediately at 1-800.....

Can a person hurt themselves from this much eye-rolling?

Phew! No Puppy Surgery!

Kramer went back to the vet this evening for his last x-ray. After 4 trips to the vet, plenty of laxatives, barium and water...he's going to be ok. No surgery needed. I'm so relieved! The flip flop has left the building.

We had to cancel our trip to Pondicherry this weekend but it was worth knowing that Kramer was going to be alright. I really didn't feel comfortable leaving him with staff.

Speaking of staff--Miss Housekeeper is going to have to be able to start taking things away from Kramer when I'm not here. If I can't trust her to take a shoe or sock away from Kramer, she'll be gone. Kramer had gotten a sock in his mouth the other day and I asked her to take it from him because I was carrying a tray. She followed him saying, "Kramer, give it to me" in a mousy voice. Yeah, that'll work. We had a discussion about keeping the laundry baskets off the floor. When I came back a half hour later, the laundry baskets were still there. I picked them up and put them on top of the washer. Hint hint.

Sista Fun

I've been having so much fun with my sister visiting that sometimes I forget where I am. I really love having her here and if she didn't have family waiting for her back home, I'd beg her to stay.

We haven't really been doing much, what with jet lag, a sick dog, the first week of middle school and Delhi belly. Hopefully, this week, we'll get out and do the whole tourist-thing. So far, we've just been hanging out in the pool and watching movies. We went for mani/pedis the other day and nearly got kicked out for being too rowdy. Apparently someone in the next room couldn't relax during their massage because we were being too loud. In all fairness, there were 10 people in a small room, the music was loud and they sat my friend clear on the other side. Once we got giggling...

In the enormous amount of stuff that my sister brought with her from Canada there were two cook books. *The Joy of Cooking* and *The Good Housekeeping Cookbook* (with step by step photos). Two excellent basic cookbooks for our cook. I had made the comment that I wished she could've brought pirogies in her suitcase (they're frozen, though). I have them every time I visit her in Alberta. We found a recipe in the *Joy of Cooking* Cookbook and all the ingredients were actually available in India to make them from scratch. It was a time-consuming process but everyone seemed to enjoy them. I know I could make them again, although it's not something I would want to do every weekend. Hmmm, maybe Mani could learn to make the pirogies?

Also in her suitcase---english muffins. JB is making eggs benedict this morning.

Who's coming to visit us next!?

Mehndi Ladies

Friday was a good India day. We booked a Mehndi[1] lady to come to the house to paint designs on our hands and feet with henna. We decided to invite a few friends over to join us. And then one can't have a gathering of ladies without a little gathering of food. That entailed simple chips and salsa, a fruit platter and some cookies. It was a ball. It was nice to see friends who were back from home leave and some new friends who had just moved to Chennai. It was fun to chat and to laugh. I think my sister had a good time too.

[1] http://en.wikipedia.org/wiki/Mehndi

Feels Like Monday

Yesterday was Independence Day in India. JB didn't go work and little man didn't have school. It was a relaxing day. We watched some movies, hung out in the pool and went out for dinner.

I'm cooking more and our cook is cooking less. I'm trying a new tactic. I'm having her do some of the prep work and a little baking. I've been handling anything to do with meat. With the amount of tummy troubles we've all had, it just seems worth it to do it myself. She was offended when I asked her to use the dishwasher instead of washing dishes by hand. She insists restaurants are what's causing my ailments. It's possible she's right but I'm not taking any chances. I've spent the last four months feeling rather cruddy. This week, I gave up and gave in to antibiotics, pain killers and other medicinal goodies.

Since yesterday felt like a weekend, I made an attempt at making Christmas Eve Shortcut Cinnamon Buns1...without the frozen dinner rolls. Connor has requested this several times since we're not doing our usual weekend at Paneras. It took three hours to make the dough from scratch and it didn't quite turn out like it does in the US, but everyone ate it with no complaints. I'm thinking if I make the dough for rolls and froze them into little ball shape sizes. It might work out properly. Anyone have advice on freezing bread dough?

We're going to try to make it to Pondicherry this weekend. Last weekend's plans were foiled by our ill puppy dog. This week, little man is supposed to have swimming on Saturday but his teacher has been kind enough to excuse him since it's his Auntie's last weekend here.

Today feels like Monday. Maybe it's because yesterday was a holiday. Maybe it's because my sister is only here for a couple more days.

1 http://www.savingdinner.com/archives/recipes/christmas_eve_shortcut_cinnamon_buns.html

The Dune, Eeeeko Hotel

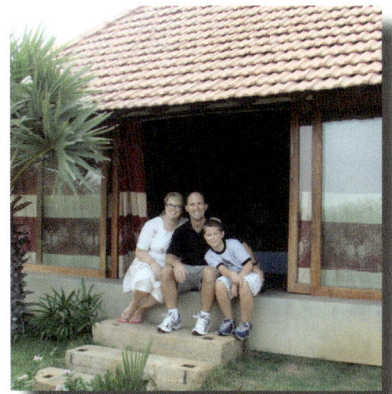

Here's where we stayed in Pondicherry--Kerala House at The Dune². It's an "eco beach resort." Allow me to translate that for you--what it really means is that it's not Danie's idea of a good time.

Let's break it down...

The Good:

- The Kerala Bungalow was an interesting 120 year old house that was shipped from Kerala and re-built on site.

- The two bedrooms were air conditioned.

- There is a pool and beach.

- It appears to be a good place to bring your bikes and ride around on the trails.

The Bad:

- Bottled water was not made available in the rooms. BYOW.

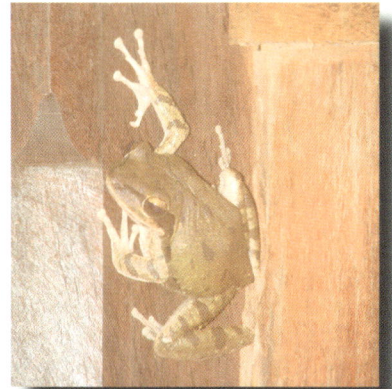

- We were too far away from the parking area to walk. We were dressed up for dinner and it was very hot. Every time we wanted to go somewhere, we had to call and wait for an electric car. And I mean *wait.*

- In the short drive via electric car, I was eaten alive by mosquitoes. The mosquitoes came back for dessert while I was sleeping.

- The eaves of the roof were open which invited all kinds of creepy crawlies in for the night.

- I'm not a fan of communing with nature. This is what greeted me when I lifted the toilet seat. I didn't see it there until it jumped from the toilet seat to the wall.

In return, I greeted "Jeremiah" with a hearty scream. And FYI, my sister took this photo because there was no way in heck I was going back into that loo. The bungalow had lovely wood work. The staff were very proud of their organic farm. This was mentioned to us at least six different times. We were invited to get up early to help with the cow milking. Those of you who know me are rolling on the floor laughing right now, I just know it. It inspired fear in me at the thought of eating at the restaurant--milk right from the cow--eww. Good thing we brought muffins and other snacks.

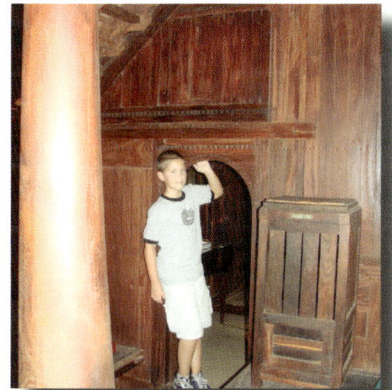

Photo Credit - Lisette W.

Apparently, the people in Kerala were on the short side 120 years ago. Here's Connor standing in one of the doorways.

I had no desire to ever ride in a rickshaw--zero. McGyver suggested I take my sister for an auto rickshaw ride while she was visiting. My reply was, "Not unless you're driving it." I was surprised when he said, "OK."

I have no idea how he managed to get his hands on an auto rickshaw but they are usually lined up and down my street because of the foreign government agency next door. He told us it would take an extra ten minutes to get to the school that day. Oh yeah, I forgot to mention that our rickshaw ride was to Connor's school to pick him up at the end of the day. And he had no idea were coming in an "auto."

We walked outside bare feet because our Mehndi wasn't dry enough to wear shoes yet. The gates opened and the auto rickshaw drove up the driveway, turned around and was ready to go. This is where the giggles started. It was an odd sight to see. And, we could've walked out the gate to get in a rickshaw. Leave it to McGyver though.

We got in. More giggling. Even McGyver was giggling. As we set off, the rickshaw was jerking back and lurching forward. More giggling. McGyver says, "Ten years past I drive an auto rickshaw." Which made me wonder what he was doing driving an auto rickshaw ten years ago. With the jerking and lurching under control, we spent the rest of the journey bumping up and down. You can really feel each crack in the road with these things. It was hot and the exhaust of the other vehicles was fairly nauseating. Been there, done that...now where's the air conditioned SUV? Kramer wasn't impressed. Chennai isn't ready for a golden retriever to be riding in an auto rickshaw so he had to stay home. I should also mention that our rickshaw was slower and louder than everyone else's. You're not going to believe this (I certainly didn't) but there are laws about how loud your rickshaw or vehicle can be in Chennai. We were worried for the whole drive that we would be stopped and ticketed. If not for the volume of the rickshaw, certainly for the volume of its passengers.

Most rickshaw drivers wear a mustard-colored uniform. The rickshaw owner left his shirt for McGyver but I can't blame him for not wanting to wear it. Lots of other rickshaw drivers were honking their horn at McGyver and waving. Apparently it was because he was wearing his white driver's uniform. Since we were in such a rowdy, giggling mood, I told him how deeply offended I was that he wasn't wearing his white driver's hat. He got a good giggle out of that too.

"Madame. Julie Madame car." My friend, who was just at my house, was ahead of us in traffic. McGyver says, "Madame. I have no pomp pomp." Meaning the rickshaw had no horn. McGyver, giggling the whole time, swerves around the motorbikes and squeezes through traffic to pull up to Julie's van. We knocked on the window, which probably scared her half to death and got our giggles on. She took more photos of us from her vehicle. Julie's driver thinks we're nuts.

When we got to school, I met Connor at the front door to help him with his bags. Rickshaws have to be parked outside the gate because they're not permitted on school property. So we casually walked out and I hopped into the rickshaw. The look on his face was priceless!

"Mom, where's the truck?"

"I traded it in for this!"

"Nuh-uh."

"Oh yeah."

"Seriously?"

"Oh yeah."

"What about that meter?"

"Well, we figured McGyver could earn a little extra cash when he picks up your friends for school." Work with me here.

"Mom! He can't charge my friends money!"

By this point, none of us could keep a straight face. "You didn't really trade in our truck, did you?" The three of us barely fit in the back seat, especially with Connor's book bag, lunch bag, swimming bag, binders etc. Definitely no room for Kramer.

On our way back home, we saw another vehicle that we recognized. Most of the expat vehicles here look the same. My friend, Michele, has an enormous American SUV. I can pick it out anywhere in any amount of traffic. So can McGyver. "Madame. Michele Madame." Again, he swerved and advanced until we were close enough to knock on her vehicle. Again, lots of giggles. The kids rolled down the window when they realized it was Connor in the rickshaw. Then they all giggled when they realized the driver was McGyver. Michele's driver thinks we're nuts too.

Between the Mehndi party and the rickshaw ride, it was the most fun day with the most laughter that I've had since I've moved here. I'm always telling Connor not to draw unnecessary attention to our vehicle by waving at people, etc. Here we were being Naughty North Americans, nay, Wild Westerners on our raucous auto rickshaw ride.

Tsk tsk.

Photo Credit Julie R.

Krishna's Butterball

Is Krishna's[1] Butterball in Mamallapuram or Mahabilapuram? Take your pick. I struggle to say either one. India is on a kick of changing street and city names. We've renamed most of the recognizable streets ourselves...Helmet Road, Tire Street, Jewelery Junction, Plumbing Blvd, etc. But the cities...

-Bombay is now Mumbai (and I agree with my sister...The Mumbai Trading Company doesn't have as nice of a ring to it)

- Madras is now Chennai

- Pondicherry is now Poducherry

- Mahabilapuram2 is now Mamallapuram[3] and it goes on and on

Anyway...according to the E-India Tourism[4] website:

> Krishna's Butterball is a huge boulder near the Ganesha Ratha. It rests precariously on a narrow rock base. It is believed that several Pallava kings have attempted to move the stone, but legend is that neither the kings nor their elephants could shift the boulder even by an inch.

We waited very patiently while native tourists casually posed in front of this massive boulder with one hand resting on the rock. How nice. No imagination, I say. I'm sure we're not the first foreigners to capture these same poses on film. Remember our photos in front of the leaning tower of Pisa? Old corny habits die hard...

A few days later, McGyver told me that several people asked him what we were doing. I thought that would be obvious. Look at the strain on Connor's face. It makes me laugh every time.

[1] http://en.wikipedia.org/wiki/Krishna

[2] http://en.wikipedia.org/wiki/Mamallapuram

[3] http://wikitravel.org/en/Mamallapuram

[4] http://www.eindiatourism.net

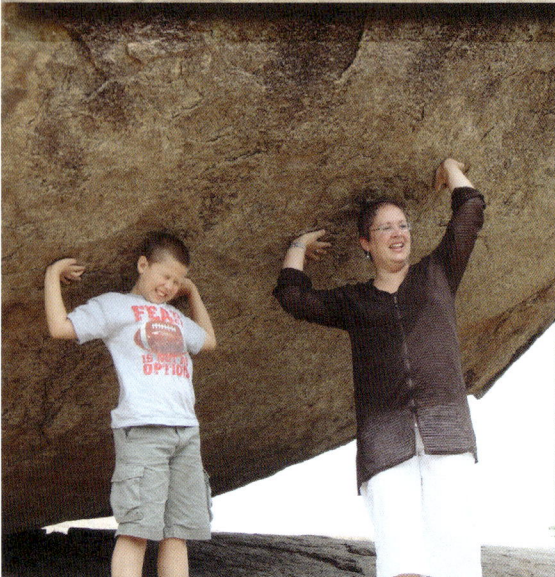

Photo Credit Lisette W.

Pondicherry Pachyderm

One of the highlights of our excursion in Pondicherry was visiting the temple area. Wherever there's a temple, there's commerce. And sensory overload.

Here is the elephant that gave his blessings: http://www.youtube.com/watch?v=9-TH52vqMAc

We did do some other touristy things while we were in Pondicherry but once we got to spend some time with the elephant, everything else was just ho-hum.

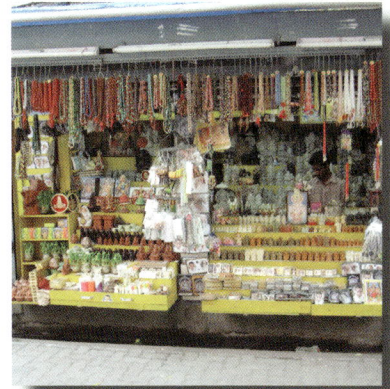

Commitment Phobias

Is it possible? Can it be? Am I ready? I've been avoiding commitment since I moved to India. I've been unfocused, have had a short attention span and always feel like I can't relax. After two really good weekends back-to-back and feeling like I'm bouncing back from my rock-bottom, I've made a few commitments. I'm scared as hell but I'm doing it anyway.

It starts with things like, yes, I can make a pasta salad for the school picnic. Yes, I'll even commit to attending the picnic. Phew. Big step. That was tough.

I've volunteered to be the middle school PTA rep at Connor's school. I have no idea what level of commitment this is. I have no idea what I'm supposed to do. I just hope I can do what I've agreed to do. I'm sure I'll be a pain in the butt to the rest of the committee with my questions. I'm a great work horse. Give me a specific task and I'll gladly complete it. I'm not so great at vague tasks that require creativity.

JB has committed the company to sponsoring a charity fundraiser event next year. It's in the form of a "ball." I know. I'm not really a ball person but I figure if the company is sponsoring it, we should probably go. I wasn't too stressed because it's over a year away. Uh-oh, hubby looks deep in thought. He says, "Do you know if I brought my tuxedo to India or was it put in storage? Wouldn't it be fun to go this year?" I'm not sure about that. I've committed to next year. This year might still be asking too much.

So, is it possible that I'm ready to jump in to my life here in Chennai? Doesn't matter. I've already leaped.

...I'd better be as good of a swimmer as I think I am!

Le Dupleix

Le Dupleix is the name of the restaurant where we had dinner in Pondicherry. While my French is quite rusty now, at one time I considered myself to be bilingual. I didn't know what *Dupleix* meant. I was pretty sure it wasn't really a valid French word so I looked it up in an online French-English Dictionary website. No such thing. I Googled the name of the restaurant and found out that it was named after Joseph Francois Dupleix[1]. So, it turns out that my French is still somewhat better than I thought; it's my history knowledge that stinks.

Everything at Le Dupleix was terrific! Well, I wouldn't order the steak again but everything else was terrific. The atmosphere, the service and the appetizers, most of the entrees were, indeed, excellent. There's also a hotel. From the brochure, it looks lovely as well. Probably none of that "eeeko" stuff going on.

The best part of dinner was that McGyver joined us. We had a good time asking all kinds of questions about his family and Indian wedding traditions. He said he "wouldn't fix his wedding date" until we get back to India after Christmas. While we didn't want to assume an invitation. We have to admit, we're very pleased about this. We would hate to miss his big day and we'd also like to spend a little time in Kerala.

Fun night!

1 http://en.wikipedia.org/wiki/Joseph_Fran%C3%A7ois_Dupleix

◀ Arachnophobia

This post is dedicated to our friend, Steve.

After the snakes and geckos, you had to know that the spiders weren't far behind. We've been having tiny black jumping spiders, but that's not such a big deal, right? Nah!

Recently, Connor found the biggest spider in our kitchen that I've ever seen in my life (outside of a zoo). It was the stuff nightmares are made of. In fact, Connor and I both had spider dreams that night.

Unfortunately, there's no reference point to give you a clear idea of how big the spider was. Suffice it to say it was bigger than the size of Connor's hand and nearly as large as mine. This photo is only slightly smaller than actual size. I have no idea if it was poisonous or not, I just wanted it out of the house. There would be no sleep until it was out or dead. All God's creatures, blah, blah, blah. Dead, I say. And I make no apologies about it.

By the time I got the photo and Connor got the broom, the spider was gone. "Oh well," says JB. Not his problem now. Only I beg to differ. Dead. Remember? I pitched a bit of a fit. How dare he think he was going to leave me at home with a massive spider so he can go to work the next day and not worry about it. I moved to India for his career. The very least he could do was to be chivalrous enough to kill a big-honkin' Indian spider for me! Personally, I didn't think I was being as unreasonable as he did.

With chair and broom in hand, and looking like he was about to fight off a lion, he went into battle while Connor held onto Kramer's collar. I was being most helpful by alternately looking on and dancing around with a severe case of the heebie jeebies. I'm so cool under pressure.

Our kitchen cabinets are hung so that they cover up a window. We suspected the spider was down behind the cabinet in the window area. Brave JB sprayed a little Raid in there and the spider flew out immediately. JB screamed in such a high pitched voice, I thought the spider had kicked him in the you-know-where. He got the spider with the broom. I have to admit that it's sort of funny to see a grown man jumping around with his broom in hand screeching over a spider--I mean, every bit as such as I would be.

With the arachnid crisis taken care of by my big, bad, brave JB, we went back upstairs to eat our pizza and watch episodes of the first season of McGyver.

I wonder how the real McGyver would handle a spider from hell.

Try the Thai

We have a favorite Thai restaurant in Chennai. Frankly, we're probably not the best people to be advertising for their restaurant since a few months ago we were sure they would ask us to not come back. I really shouldn't share any of this--which makes it all the more reason why I will.

Our friend was visiting from the US. He was here on business but he spent his whole day off helping us move and unpack boxes. Yeah, what a guy, huh? Oh! And it was his birthday, too! We took him to dinner for Thai. Well, we tried to. We sat down and ordered a bottle of water. They brought us cold towels to wash our hands before dinner. Connor had Delhi Belly (really bad) and decided we really should go home--and right away. So we paid for our water, left a huge tip and exited the restaurant very quickly. When we got home, we realized that Connor had left with the facecloth in his hand. Doh! My kid, the thief.

Like we weren't embarrassed enough! When we finally worked up enough courage to go back, here's what happened…We were goofing around at the table. I agree, we shouldn't have been. It was completely inappropriate. We got to laughing so hard I could barely breathe. The whole time, JB was glaring at me across the table. I kept laughing uncontrollably. I just couldn't make myself stop. If there's one thing I can pretty much guarantee, I'm going to laugh when it's especially inappropriate to do so. You should see me in a formal church. Yikes! As Connor went to take a sip of water, I bumped his elbow. And maybe it was a little bit on purpose. I know. It's positively shameful. Instead of the water merely pouring down his chin as I had intended, he began to choke. I admit it, I'm a horrible mother. Suffice it to say, the end result was ugly. It felt like it took forever to get and pay our check. We were so ashamed. We didn't dare *ever* go back.

The lure of the Thai food proved to be too much. We considered other Thai restaurants but we really like *this* one--and it's right down the street from where we live. It took at least a month before I went back with a friend for lunch to feel out management. They greeted me warmly. Maybe they didn't remember? Not likely. But their graciousness impressed me and shamed me.

It was a long time again after that before we first went back for dinner as a family. When we finally did, we were chosen to appear in an online video advertisement. We weren't expecting to be asked hard questions, but the truth is, we don't know the names of any of the dishes. Nor can we pronounce reading them off the menu. We just point and order our favorites.

We've been back regularly with friends and family members since all the drama. And I promise, we're always on our very best behavior and always leave really big tips!

http://chennailive.in/chennailive_morevideos.
php?video=14490638%7C14491186

Where's the Dung?

Quite often, as we crawl into bed for the night, we will share an observation or funny incident from our day. Last night, hubby told me about a woman he saw on his way to work. In one hand, she was carrying a jug of water. In her other hand, she was carrying a nicely rounded, large ball of dung.

That led us to think…there are cows on every corner, there are ox-pulled carts in the streets, you'd think there would be more droppings everywhere. After living in India for nearly 6 months, our inquiring minds would like to know, "Where's the Dung?"

Here's the answer: http://en.wikipedia.org/wiki/
Cow_dung

Only on this blog, will you read a serious post about cow poop.

Sizzling Brownie

You've heard me talk about it. The Sizzling Brownie. Is it God's perfect food? Probably. Forget everything you've ever heard about the banana being the perfect food. Last time I checked, the banana has zero effect on a bad day. See, that's where the Sizzling Brownie comes in.

My friend, Stephanie, so graciously saved me from having to eat the whole dessert by myself. What are friends for, huh? It takes a long time to cool down but I always dig in before it's cool enough and burn my tongue anyway. Same stupid behavior repeated with the same results. Duh.

So, where do you find this yummy concoction? The Cream Center on Chaimers Rd.

Tell 'em Danie sent you.

When Life Pukes On You

...and I mean that quite literally.

Hubby was having a rough day. I don't envy the man. His job is very stressful and nearly impossible to do. As usual, it started out with more bad news at work. Then it just went downhill from there.

He generally spends between 3-4 hours per day in the car...on a good day. Meaning it isn't raining, there have been no traffic accidents or the Chief Minister's path is not crossing with his. Basically, the stars have to align for a good traffic day. This afternoon, he called me on his way home from work as he usually does. This time though, the horns were much louder than usual. He was calling me from outside the car. Don't you just know that if your day starts cruddy, there's probably nothing but more crud on the way.

Immediately, I was very concerned. Something had to be wrong. He informed me that he was standing in the middle of the road in a very rural area outside Chennai. Why on earth would that be?

Well, Elvis (JB's driver) was off today due to a death in the family. The relief driver vomited all over himself. They pulled over, he cleaned up, got water and said he was good to go again. A little ways down the road, he vomited again--all over himself and the car...while driving. JB convinced him to pull the car over and got out. The driver, once he was feeling better, got in the car and drove away leaving hubby standing on the side of the road to wait for a ride.

He called for McGyver, but McGyver had to battle traffic to get out there to pick him up. Luckily, McGyver arrived before the looming black clouds opened up. That wouldn't have been pretty. Especially considering hubby was on his way to a business dinner.

What a way to whet an appetite, huh?

On another note, which has nothing to do with puke whatsoever...

When I got home from school today, The King came running over (as usual) with something report. Today, it's that the company is adding a little more BAM to our security. I'm already the laughing stock among my non-company friends who already think we have too much security as it is. Metal detectors will be used on staff and anyone else who comes through the gate. I've asked that this not be used on my friends (how embarrassing), which The King has agreed to. I did tell him that I thought it would funny to pull the metal-detector routine on our landlords on their next snooping mission. Naughty Danie! On top of all that, the company has also arranged another security assessment for our property.

I'm grateful that we're being well taken care of and that the company is looking out for our safety. This does all seem like a little much though. I have to admit that it makes me wonder if something is going on that I'm not aware of. Yet.

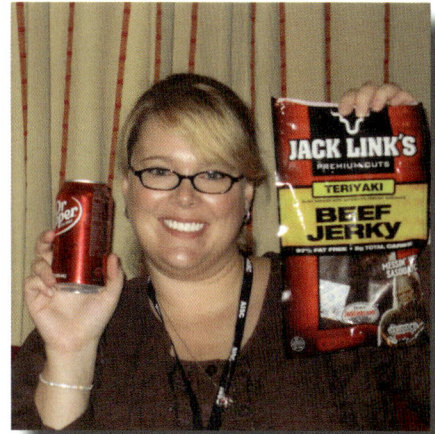

Wouldn't you like to be a Pepper too?

Oh happy day! Our food shipment arrived. All those glorious boxes...plus two proper mops. Phone calls and text messages were flying to see who had the most boxes, what kind of shape the boxes were in and to compare notes on the first treats everyone dug into. One friend[1] was so happy and emotional--I think she was actually crying! I can't blame her though. She's lived here a long time without a food shipment. And it's like Christmas when this stuff comes through the door.

In this house, the first treats were beef jerky and Dr. Pepper for me. Rold Gold mini pretzels and Dr. Pepper for Connor. Husband went straight for the mini Chips Ahoy (Penny had carte blanche at Sam's Club). Milkbones for Kramer. There was real food in those boxes too but we each picked a treat first. Now comes the job of unpacking the boxes and organizing the pantry.

THANK YOU for the treats, Miss Penny! You did one heck of a job!

So far, we haven't opened all the boxes but it doesn't look like customs did their usual damage. And, so far, they've only taken one juice box. I hope they didn't take our maple syrup again!

[1] http://julieandsteve.blogspot.com/2007/09/food-has-arrived.html

R.I.P. Michael

When we first moved here, we had a guard named Michael. I believe he was from northern India or Nepal. He was friendly and we liked him. Unfortunately, he was regularly sleeping during his shift, even on day shift. Due to our insistence that he stay awake during work, one day he stormed out in the middle of his shift. Our head guard thought that he may have been doing drugs. Michael went to the RM (regional manager) and asked for another post. He was posted a few doors down from where we live, and after three warnings, he ended up being put on suspension for sleeping on duty. When he went to the RM's office at the end of his suspension, he went with an attitude and the RM fired him.

Michael demanded money from his boss for being fired (you fired me, you owe me) and he was refused. That night, he sold his watch for Rs.100. He bought a bottle of wine and a box of rat poison. He mixed the two and drank all of it. He told his friends that the next day was his birthday and his death day. He went to the roof of his building. He either jumped or fell off the roof, killing himself.

His body was brought to the hospital while his parents traveled three days to come and claim him. He was not embalmed, so three days later after being left in the heat...I can't imagine the state he was in when his parents got to see him. What a horrible thing to endure. When his parents arrived, Michael had been stripped of everything. Even his clothes had been taken. There was no bag of personal effects. They requested a sheet or something to wrap him in so he could be moved with dignity and they were denied. Then they were asked to leave.

Michael was the only son in his family. He was also the only child who could support his parents, as is typically done in India. There are 1800 guards at the security company who each gave Rs.10 to the parents, totaling about $450 US dollars.

I pray that Michael finds the peace he wasn't able to find on earth.

The Fired Gardener

This is--scratch that-- **was** our gardener. Remember back in July, I told you about people wearing bags on their heads when its rains? This was the second time I had seen the gardener wearing a bag on his head. The first time, it was yellow. But the second time, being pink, I couldn't resist snapping a photo. He smiles like that all the time!

Here's the story of the fired gardener...

Look at the photo. See the wall? That wall surrounds the whole property. Remember the garbage outside the wall? It's all been cleaned up.

New grass and plants were planted. When the topic of maintaining the landscaping came up, the gardener says, "That's not my job."

We insisted that being the gardener, the garden inside and outside the gate is his job. He asked for a raise because it's more work. My response was, "Are you planning on working more hours?"

"No." No raise.

He was already being paid more than any other gardener in our neighborhood. *And* he was only doing an actual two hours of work per day. He was sleeping, having coffee breaks and hanging out with one of his wives outside our gate.

Look at the wall again. See all the mold and mildew along the top? I asked the gardener to work on cleaning it. "Not my job," he said. This was followed by a whole lot of back-and-forth discussion. Then it was ended with...Fine. "I'll clean it myself. But if I do, I'll have no reason to be paying you to stand there watching me do your job." By the end of the conversation, I was very frustrated. I got to the point where if I want something done right, I'm going to have to do it myself.

Yesterday morning, I woke up with a head full of steam. I put on my grubbies, grabbed the ladder, bucket, hose and scrub brush. Away I went. The guards informed me how embarrassed they were that madame was doing such labor. They offered to help, but I declined. The drivers offered to help. I declined. The pool guy offered to help. I declined. I did take him up on his offer to obtain some chlorine for me though since I was running out of the Tilex that I had imported in our shipment.

The gardener didn't show up for work that day. He did come around sometime in the afternoon to negotiate his job. There was no negotiating. He didn't have a job anymore. I explained that it wasn't the guards' job to clean the wall. It wasn't the drivers' job either. It certainly wasn't Pool Guy's job. But they were all willing to do it. His argument is that we didn't specify that particular task when we hired him. We sure didn't. Then again, how was I to know that 5 months later, the wall was going to turn moldy? I didn't. Be flexible buddy...you were hired for *gardening and light maintenance*.

I could've taken my time to complete the task but I went hard at it, completing one whole wall. Today, I can barely move. My back, arms and legs are screaming! Thankfully, by the end of the day, we had hired a new "all-in-all" to handle gardening, maintenance and being flexible enough to handle whatever else may come up.

The lessons learned yesterday:

- When madame says something, she really does mean it.

- Madame doesn't expect anyone to do anything she isn't willing to do herself.

- Madame expects people to do their jobs and earn their pay.

- Madame is tougher than she looks.

- And, it's best to stay out of madame's way when she has a full head of steam.

- Most importantly...be flexible.

Class dismissed!

Happy Birthday to Me!

And it's not even my birthday! My birthday was three months ago. This is the package that my mom sent three and a half months ago with hopes of it arriving by my birthday.

We have a tradition. We always call the person who sent a package so we can open it while we're on the phone with them. It was 3:20AM in Canada and I was dying to dial the phone. I knew she'd have a heart attack. If the phone rang in the middle of the night, she would think something is wrong.

Honestly, I figured this package was long gone. I knew someone out there was enjoying my goodies. I took some cruddy photos with my mobile phone camera and tore into it. In that order. 'Cause I know it looks like I tore into it, and *then* decided to take photos.

The box was no longer sturdy, but it didn't look like anyone opened it. In fact, I know nobody opened it or the maple lollipops wouldn't have still been in there!

I should mention that my mother didn't wrap the ropes around the package. That was done somewhere en route. The ropes weren't tied they were fastened with what looked like globs of tar (or something). She had been nagging Canada Post (as only a mother can) every week about where the package was. It had a tracking number but it indicated that for 3 months, it hadn't left Canada. You can always count on Canada Post.

There was a little something in there for everyone. Connor was so excited when I told him, he couldn't wait to get home from school. There's a new outfit in there that he's keeping for his first middle school dance on Friday night.

JB munched on the Smarties all afternoon during his phone conferences. Whenever a care package arrives, he snoops for the Smarties right away! My mother has shipped Smarties to every country and state we've lived in.

After a long hard day of cleaning the mold off the outside walls, this care package was quite a treat!

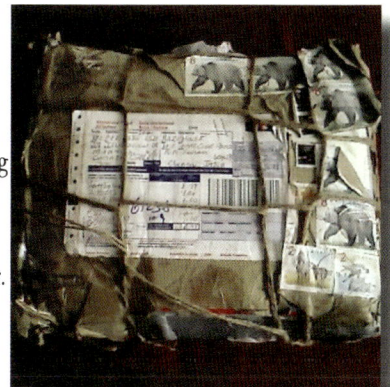

Sri Lanka: The Arrival & First Impressions

Hi! We're back from Sri Lanka but I wrote blog posts while I was away. This is what I do when I'm awake 3 hours before everyone else in the hotel room and I'm trying to be quiet. And, all the upcoming Sri Lanka blog posts were typed on my PDA thumb-keyboard. That's dedication for ya, folks.

So here we are in Colombo, Sri Lanka. It's cleaner and it's greener. We were met at the airport by our driver. The first thing he says when we get into the van is, "The traffic and drivers are very crazy in Sri Lanka." Obviously this guy has never been to India. People cross the streets at crosswalks. They hold out their hand and traffic stops for them. Every head on a motorbike wears a helmet. Cars are operated in their traffic lane. There's no livestock in the street. I haven't even seen anyone peeing in the streets. What has happened to me when I think that's a normal thing? The only crazy going on in Colombo traffic is the crazy pleasure we derived from experiencing it!

Sri Lanka is 69% Buddhist (so the driver told us). There are many temples and mini prayer temples (as I call them) along the road. It was different to see them filled mostly with Buddha statues and a few Christian ones with Mary and baby Jesus. We haven't seen one Ganesh. So far.

The hotel is lovely and the food at the Italian restaurant on site has been yum--no five spice. It just reiterates to me that these regular jaunts out of India are very important to my sanity. Although I think my preference for relaxation wouldn't involve armed soldiers in the future.

Call me a freak, but military check points with automatic weapons, bunkers and the overall defensive aura makes me a little edgy. I wasn't expecting that.

JB and Connor are cooling off in the pool (it's hotter and more humid here). Personally, I'm going opt for a proper bath in a proper big bath tub. Yee. Haw.

Sri Lanka: SAISA Day 1

International schools from Chennai, Delhi, Dhaka, Katmandu and Mumbai gathered at the Colombo school for the swim competition. The opening ceremony treated us to a performance of local dance and the team captains lighting a lantern.

Connor only had one race on day 1, 100m freestyle. He was disappointed that he placed 14th. We were pleased for him that he shaved 5 seconds off his personal best time. He spent the rest of the day cheering for his team mates. It was a long day, which to our dismay, was followed up by a dance. We were told on several occasions that study times were built into SAISA events. When our day starts at 6am and finishes at 9:30pm there's no time for drum practice, math or reading.

Not many parents traveled here to see their kids compete. I was very surprised by that. Mumbai had a large crowd of parents and I was impressed by their cohesiveness and spirit. We've met most of the parents...nice crowd.

We took advantage of the lunch break and went to the local country club. We sat facing the 18th hole of a lovely golf course and enjoyed a fine meal. We miss golf. I miss *pretty*. The Japanese teppanyaki won our vote for dinner. We chatted about the day and found that the overall feeling in Sri Lanka makes it easier to relax than in Chennai. It seems to be a happier culture and the local people take pride in their country.

In chatting with expats this weekend we discovered something interesting that we've not noticed in the past. The same questions always come up in expat chat. Where do you live? Where are you from? How long have you been an expat? Where have you been posted? There seems to be a growing attitude among expats of whether you're 'expat enough.' Twelve years as an expat is 'less expat' than 25 years with the kids being born all around the world. You might also be 'more expat' than someone else if your posts have been tougher. A post in India would make us 'more expat' than our England or US posts? Seriously. Expat is expat. You're still away from home. *sigh*

As I looked around the pool area at the visiting teams and the Colombo kids who came by to cheer between classes, I was struck by the thought that every one of these kids is either living away from the home they knew or living a life that has never known a long-term home with roots. They were all expats. They were all from schools with large numbers of additional expats. They were all like us. I'm amazed at how many cities around the world have international schools and how many kids attend these schools. And the parents of all these children have dealt with all the same stuff that, as expats, we deal with.

Most people live in their communities. Our community is spread all over the world.

Sri Lanka - SAISA Day 2

We're done. I'm too hot and too tired to give it the *yahoo* it deserves. It's been two long, hot, fun days.

Today, Connor did the 50m freestyle (3 second improvement), 50m breast stroke and the 13-14 year 100m x 4. That's right, I said 13-14 year age group. Connor's 10. While it was exciting for him to swim in that event and it allowed him to take home a medal (6th place), it was also a test of sportsmanship skills to his team mates. They knew they were going to come in last with a 10 year old on their relay team and their disappointment was obvious. Connor overheard their whinging and he felt bad. All swimmers have a first year competing. This was his.

And we're so proud him! We're proud of him for waking up early every morning and going to all his swim practices...some weeks he put in extra practices. We're proud of him for working hard and improving in all his events...up to 30 seconds over two months in some of them. We're proud that gave it his all.

A few more parents showed up today so we had a good cheering section. We cheered for every Chennai swimmer. Most of us went back to the local country club for lunch again. It was nice to spend some time getting to know them. The general consensus was that Colombo is paradise compared to Chennai...as we were sitting on the 18th hole of a lovely golf course eating regular food.

Now I wouldn't say that Colombo is paradise. Most of our family and friends who have never traveled to Asia would be stunned by the contrast to their home country. It's all relative, though. It is, indeed, nicer than Chennai. I'd come back again as long as it remains safe to do so. Only I'd bring my golf clubs next time. I really would get to the Elephant Orphanage as I had hoped, but didn't get to do this time.

So, all in all it was a nice experience and given the opportunity we would participate again. And again. Go Raptors!

Sri Lanka - Sunday and The Haircut

Sunday: The swim team met at Odel's[1] for a little retail therapy. It was a nice department store slash mall...It wasn't really clearly defined. Maybe it was a dept. store with additional shops within? Dunno. We picked up a few souvenirs and took advantage of the Deli France Café.

Since we were on a shopping roll we decided to try a couple of other places as well. We treated Connor to another Nintendo DS since his first one was stolen in Illinois and his replacement DS was jacked in Chennai. He was really pleased. These things aren't easy to find in this part of the world. This one was imported to Sri Lanka from Dubai. We also hit a book store and picked up a good guide book...ok, and a few trashy light reads. Mom was happy too.

There were a few other shops on our list to check out but the Sri Lankan version of Delhi Belly took over, which I've dubbed "Colombo Colon." Meds, nap, high tea, bunco, happy hour, steak dinner, bath, early bed...that was how the rest of the day played out.

Tomorrow morning, I may try to squeeze in a little time at the hotel salon for a power pamper before we leave for the airport and return to reality. Ugh, I'm already dreading it.

Monday: How many Sri Lankans does it take for a hair cut? The truth? 13--1 to wash , 1 to turn the radio to Eminem , 1 to cut , 1 to sweep , 6 to randomly take turns touching the hair , 5 to watch. Closely.

So much for the power-pamper. I had time for a hair cut and that was it. I'm really low maintenance about my hair. I have very little vanity when it comes to hair. But, I hadn't had a hair cut in six months. I had been holding out for Home Leave, but it became an emergency. I looked terrible. My philosophy has always been…a bad hair cut, ehn, the hair will grow back.

I've had bad hair cuts before. I've had bad hair color before (ie: green hair when it was supposed to be blond). Today, my low-vanity hair philosophy was tested.

It was the first time I can ever recall having a girl-size hissy fit about my hair. I had it cut at the hotel salon. It was a nice 5 star chain hotel and the salons in these places are usually a safe bet for expats. And really, nobody could make my hair look much worse than what it was, anything would definitely be an improvement. Um. Right.

I asked for a chin-length cut, demonstrating with my hands a straight bob cut. I asked for side swept bangs. I went out on a limb and told him I would need an "undercut." I explained that an undercut was cutting the bottom layer slightly shorter so the ends would turn under instead of flipping out. "Yes, yes, I know undercut madam." Terrific. His English was excellent and he seemed to understand my simple cut. Um. Right.

He *hacked* the back of my hair off. It's all mushroom in the back with the sides sloping longer than the back. I didn't realize what he was doing back there. I was distracted by the number of spectators. When he held up the mirror to show me (when the haircut was complete) I thought I was going to start to cry…which, is really not like me. I don't cry about hair. I don't care one iota about hair. How could I be on the edge of tears? The hair looks like it should be on tarty Posh Spice. It's just not me. It's too high-maintenance and I'm way more plain Jane than that!

I went back to our room so I could have a five minute tantrum. Five minutes was all I needed to see if I could do something that would allow me to live with it and regain my composure. The door was locked. JB and Connor had taken our bags and checked out. They were waiting for me in the lobby with our airport transfer. This was serious. I couldn't have my brush, hairspray and my tantrum. Darn. I was going to have my tantrum on the way to the airport. I really hate this kind of multi-tasking, but there was no way to avoid the ride to the airport and my meltdown was imminent.

Poor JB and Connor. They had to endure it. And there's nothing worse than being placated in the middle of a melt down. Luckily, (and screw dieting) there was plenty of duty-free chocolate and ice-blended coffee drinks at the airport. *Sigh* and my world was nearly right again. Fine, I'm a chocolate floozy. Whatever. It didn't fix the bad hair but I'm getting over it. It will grow out. Maybe even enough to have something done to it on Home Leave. Um. Right.

[1] http://www.odel.lk/?page=home

Hospital Tour

Oooo, it is really tough coming back to Chennai. It has taken a few days to ease back into it. The drivers and guards thought I was ill because they hadn't seen me for three days. Of course I must be sick, it would never occur to them that I would just like to be left alone. Traveling is a double-edged sword. We have to travel so we can get out of Chennai, feel normal and relax. But coming back is tough! Connor was back to school for one day when he came home with conjunctivitis, he has a loose tooth, and his stomach problems still haven't been solved by the company doctor, so today we went to see a Gastroenterologist.

When we moved here, all the other expats had recommended to us that we use the Apollo hospitals and clinics. After 15 minutes in the car, I knew we weren't going to Apollo. It was a 45 minute drive to the hospital. It was almost all the way out to JB's workplace. The company doctor set up the appointment and met us at the hospital.

Before our appointment, we had a conversation about what our limit of treatment would be at the hospital. Connor has been having stomach problems for 4 or 5 months. He's had several courses of treatment and nothing has worked. At least no more than short term. I had a hunch that they would want to do an endoscopy (private hospital, multi-national company expat--oh yeah). It makes me uncomfortable on many different levels. We'll start with another course of meds. After a week, if things haven't improved, he'll have an ultrasound. I can live with that. If they feel he needs a scope, we're out of here, but I'll cross that bridge when we get to it.

So, we were sitting in the examination room. Me, JB, Connor, the specialist, the company doctor, a hospital escort, along with the guest & media relations representative. That's right, I said 7 people. Thank God it wasn't a OB/GYN appointment for me!! When the examination was complete, the fun began...word got out there was a different kind of MD in the hospital. We had a tour of the hospital (nod, smile, repeat) and were shown the area of rooms set aside for their VIP patients. Seriously, they were apartments that included a living area, dining area, separate sleeping area for family, kitchen, two bathrooms. Nonetheless, there were still geckos...eek! I wouldn't hesitate to have treatment for a broken arm, chest x-ray and whatever light treatment that would be needed. I seriously doubt that I would have anything invasive done though. As were sitting in an office waiting for Connor's meds to arrive, the lady that had given us the tour started telling an Indian couple in her office that the "Americans" (meaning us) think India is dirty (we didn't say that, but, um, yeah...it is). She tells them that she is trying to show us that Indian hospitals are on par with American ones. What could we say? I'm not going to get into all the reasons why what she said about us is true, although we tried not to give that impression while we were there. Nod, smile, repeat.

Telling me that something is cheap is never a good selling point for me. I believe that when it comes to medical care (er, and diamonds), you get what you pay for. There is no such thing as a bargain diamond, you pay less for less quality. Same goes with health care. We were told that people come from Dubai and from all over the middle east to receive treatment at this hospital because it's cheap. Yay, for them. Would you have Lasik Surgery on your eyes at one place over another simply because it was cheaper? Another "selling point" was that the free clinic for the poor didn't smell bad. "Would you like to see it?" There we were, smiling like idiots, but not nodding. We had already spent a couple of uncomfortable hours there and JB had to get to work. We saw no other visible foreigners in the building...probably not a good sign. As soon as we left, Connor and I both reached for the antibacterial hand sanitizer at the same time.

I'm ready for our next trip. Just 6 weeks to go. 2 months, 1 week and 1 day until Home Leave. I can make it!

Cultural Differences

Living in India, we experience a barrage of cultural differences on a daily basis. I was surprised this week when I experienced a cultural gap with a different nationality of expats.

We were discussing a proposed middle school event. When I first heard about the event I felt very uncomfortable about it. I couldn't really articulate why the idea was outside my comfort zone so I sounded like an idiot when I tried to explain it. I was asked to get some feedback from other parents. I talked to two American moms who instantly said, "No way." I asked them to hear me out. I gave them all the finer details, and softened, I got a "Not likely." Fair enough. I met with a couple of other moms (from a different region of the globe) who thought it was a great idea. And I was surprised that they didn't seem to have any misgivings about it at all. By the end of the meeting, I got the feeling that these women thought I was a crack-pot over-protective mom. Maybe I am.

I tried to see it from their point of view. I tried to imagine myself in their shoes. I tried to imagine what life is like in their countries. I was very curious. They were coming from the point of view of--kids need independence. The Americans were coming from the point of view of--kids need to be protected. Both are absolutely right, of course. But it made me wonder how these two regions on the globe differ culturally, differ in types and quantity of crime. How is life the same or different?

The conclusion was to go ahead, plan the event (sometime in the future and try a smaller event first) and let parents decide whether or not their kids would be permitted to attend. I struggled with...should the school be making this decision or should the parents? The bottom line is that I can't control what the school does. I can't control what the parents do.

Being a minority North American at the school, my choices all come down to me. I choose what I feel is appropriate for our son based on my own upbringing, my mish-mash of cultural experiences and my own religious beliefs. It was freeing to come to the realization that I don't have to control this event, and believe me, I don't want to.

I can just say no, and agree to disagree.

Parrys Corner

Oh yes I did. And I made it back to blog about it.

I went to Parrys Corner today. Not just the main roads either, I went deep into the Georgetown and Broadway areas. Deep. Oh yeah, I did. Not long ago a woman told me that people here like to say Parrys Corner fast so it sounds like "Paris Corner." Parrys and Paris have nothing in common, trust me. I went there to find some polyester webbing and plastic clips for a little project I'm working on. I found most of what I was looking for but not before I:

- was stared at, gawked at, and followed through the streets out of interest.

- was pushed and shoved.

- had a breast grazed (and more than once).

- had my backside groped (I may not have seen who did it but I sure as heck felt it).

- was spit on (wrong place at the wrong time).

- paid too much for the items I needed.

- had to buy everything in larger quantities than everyone else.

- had a growing audience behind me while I made my purchases.

- was hit by a delivery truck...I should have a good bruise on my arm to show for it.

- was not asked for money once! No beggars! I was surprised and pleased by this.

- thought a thousand times, what on earth am I doing here?

- gagged several times due to the amount of exhaust and various other pungent aromas wafting in the air.

- realized how desperate I would have to be before I ever went back again.

Seriously, it was way more wild and woolly than Pondy Bazaar or Richie Street. I was half running (wearing flip-flops) to keep up with McGyver but trying to not get my toes run over or get hit by a bike, motorcycle, rickshaw or delivery truck...oops, I failed at that one, I got hit anyway! And if you know me at all, you know what a klutz I am. I cannot be trusted to walk without falling over and breaking my arm...oops, been there done that! Therefore, I couldn't even stop for a split second to take a picture or a video clip. I would have loved to though! You just wouldn't believe how crowded, busy and noisy this place was! I would've never have found the items I was looking for, nor would I have found my way back to the truck without McGyver. While it would be grossly inappropriate, it was all I could to do to not grab on to him and not let go. Thankfully, he was mindful of when I wasn't aggressive enough to keep up with him and he patiently stopped to wait for me.

That's enough trauma for one day (um, week...month??). I think I'll go sneak a bite of chocolate and lay down for a bit in a dark, quiet room until I recover from sensory overload.PS...When I got up from my rest, I found everything I needed on eBay (in Hong Kong). I should have just done that to begin with! Nobody ever gets a boob groped on eBay!

...As did the witch who showed up at my door before hand. Our local chapter of the Overseas Women's Club organized Halloween trick-or-treating in our neighborhood. For some reason, I had it on my calendar for Friday. Imagine my surprise when a witch arrived at my door to ask if I was still planning on participating (on Thursday). Seriously, I whipped up Halloween at the front gate in less ten minutes! I threw the lanterns to Connor to hang on the gate, the balloons to McGyver to blow up and the candy to the guards to sort out. Voila. Halloween Indian-style.

Kudos to my pal, Penny, who is the rock-star of shopping. Without her, there would have been no Halloween at all! We were expecting 120 kids and I was able to prepare for 140. I rummaged through the pantry and pulled together enough individual bags of chippies, Ritz Bits, pretzels and Oreos.. Not to mention the 5lbs bag of Tootsie Rolls and case of Starburst candies that got tossed in with the toffee candies that the OWC provided.

Connor was a little disappointed that he didn't get to dress up and make the tour. I think he understood after handing out the treats. He was a good sport and did a good job too, especially considering his low tolerance for young kids. If we were in the US, he would have still participated. But here, it just wasn't in the cards. I think he felt a bit gypped.

I didn't get to prepare the staff for the ghoulish event since I was a bit behind on preparations. I asked The King what he thought when the lady showed up dressed as a witch. He thought the long stringy white hair was her own. McGyver clearly loves little kids. He was ushering them in and helping them open their bags. I offered the staff some candy and The King said he only wanted soft candy (he doesn't have a full set of teeth, bless his heart). McGyver pipes up, "All the candy is soft after five minutes." True enough. It was very hot and humid.

Most of the ghosts and goblins were not from countries where Halloween is celebrated. Here are the cutest trick-or-treaters that came our way...Sophia, Avalon and Magnus. These kids seriously made my day. Sophia liked to pick out the pink candies and she blew kisses like a real princess. Avalon didn't need her tiger hood, she has a head full of orange curls under there. I think Magnus was eating the candy as he collected it from each house. Their parents were more excited than they were over the American treats being doled out chez-nous.

While I'm on the topic. Here are some questions from abroad: Will you celebrate Halloween in India? In the community or in Connor's school? Do they celebrate "US" holidays?

The international school did have some Halloween activities for the elementary grades. Only a few American holidays are observed by the school. A draft copy of next year's schedule has been released and I don't think any American (or Canadian for that matter) is too impressed that there's a whole week off for Diwali but not even a day for Thanksgiving. I think Thanksgiving is important. I'd gladly give up the Halloween festivities to celebrate Thanksgiving. This was actually brought up at our last PTA meeting. But the international folks seem to think that Thanksgiving is a religious holiday, not a historical one. The school is becoming less American and more international. So there you have it. Halloween in India. We'll be celebrating Diwali in Dubai, maybe. And Christmas in Canada.

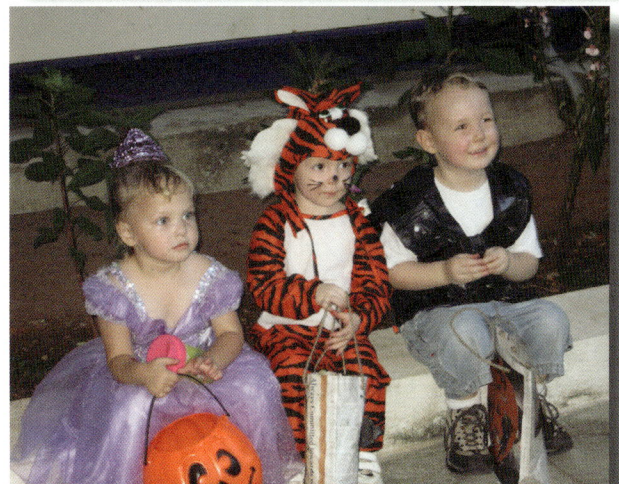

Vocab 101

I enjoy reading other people's blogs. Especially blogs of other expats in India. Yesterday, I read a blog post written by an Indian about American expats living in India. Did you follow that? Anyway, I'd like to make one thing very clear.

> Expatriate:
>
> : to withdraw (oneself) from residence in one's native country.

...does not mean the same as...

> Ex-patriot:
>
> : one who does not love his or her country and does not support its authority and interests

That's all I have to say about that.

Ayudha Pooja

I woke up early and came into my office to read (since the internet was down again). I heard a sound I knew to be sweeping but knew nobody would be sweeping at 5:30am. I looked out the window and the guards had removed all the furniture from the guardhouse. They were sweeping the floor and washing down the front gate. Serious preparations for the Ayudha Pooja. McGyver asked us if we could have a Pooja (can also be spelled Puja). It seemed important to him and interesting to us, so we agreed.

> The Ayudha Puja is a worship of whatever implements one may use in one's livelihood. On the preceding evening, it is traditional to place these implements on an altar to the Divine. If one can make a conscious effort to see the divine in the tools and objects one uses each day, it will help one to see one's work as an offering to God. It will also help one to maintain constant remembrance of the divine. In India it is customary for one to prostrate before the tools one will use before starting one's work each day; this is an expression of gratitude to God for helping one to fulfil one's duties. -Durga Puja website. (http://www.durga-puja.org/ayudha-puja.html)

Our front gate was decorated and Kolams (http://en.wikipedia.org/wiki/Kolam) were created on the ground at the threshold.

So it turns out our new gardener used to be a hindu priest. He performed the Pooja, assisted by Kasturi and McGyver. Connor and I had no idea what to expect! There was an altar set up in the guardhouse with pictures of Ganesh, flowers and food offerings. The gardening tools were laid on the floor in front of the altar. We all received blessings and had fired waved around us to ward off evil spirits. All of the staff followed with the exception of JB's driver (he's Christian). I should point out that we're Christian too. We don't believe in Hindu gods, ganesh, etc. It made our staff happy to have this pooja and it also made them happy for us to participate. By no means does it indicate any belief in this on our part.

In addition, all sides of our house and back-up power generator were blessed. The cars were decorated with flowers. All of the bicycles belonging to the staff were decorated. They even brought our bicycles out of the garage and lined them up with their own. The cars, motorbikes and bicycles were blessed. Lemons were placed in front of each of the tires of the bikes and cars. At the end of the Pooja, they ushered us into the car so we could drive over the lemons. We drove around the block and came back. A pumpkin (that's what they called it but it looked like a watermelon to me) was smashed in front of our gate.

We went out for lunch after the Pooja and saw smashed watermelons in front of nearly every gate throughout town. JB had attended a Pooja at work on Friday. Although it was a day off for all the staff, they came in for the Pooja and to receive gift bags. Someone asked him if we had taken care of the gift bags for our staff. Wha??? Man, I wish I knew this kind of stuff in advance. In the end we got it sorted. After our Pooja, JB handed out gift bags to all the staff.

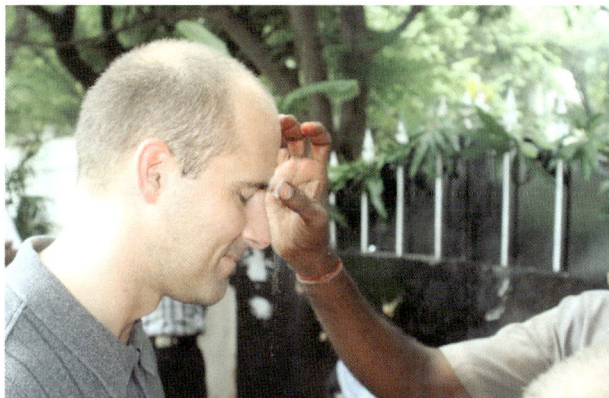

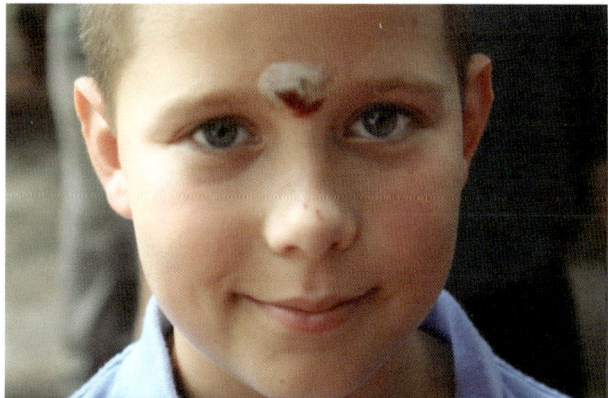

Monsoon

The weather forecast for the next 10 days...rain.

Here it comes.

Canadian Winter vs. Indian Monsoon

I left the house today to go to a local hotel. It usually takes 15-20 minutes to get there. Except I forgot that the streets may be flooded.

As we were held up in traffic I began to think that Indian Monsoon is really no different than a Canadian Winter as they both have two things in common...

1) Both the snow and rain wreak havoc on traffic.

2) Kids like to bundle up to play in the snow or strip down to play in the puddles. And they have an equal amount of fun.

I wish I had the presence of mind to snap a photo of three little kids splashing around in a huge puddle, naked as could be. They were having a blast!

So, rain is to India as snow is to Canada.

Fair Prices on the Fairways

As our family and friends are beginning to think about putting their clubs away for the fall/winter, we're just beginning to look at pulling ours out again. Last week I decided I was going to get some info about playing golf in Chennai. JB was doing his phone conferences from home and I asked if he had the time to come with me. No. Half way to the golf course I knew I was kidding myself. This was going to be an exercise in frustration. Why do that to myself? I had McGyver turn the car around to take me home. I would just wait until "sir" was free to come with me. Saturday was the day. We drove out to the golf course. We had been told many times by many different people not to expect much. So I went there expecting brown dusty fairways. Actually, I couldn't tell you what the fairways or the greens looked like because I didn't get out of the car.

When we pulled up to the gate, our vehicle was rushed by 30 or so men and young boys. It completely freaked me out. McGyver unlocked the doors so JB could get out and before I knew what was happening, someone from the crowd was opening my door. I pulled the door closed and locked it. Connor was scared. I was scared. McGyver was humored. These were the (very aggressive) caddy-wannabees. We parked the car across the street. They continued to swarm around JB hoping to be the one he chose to carry his golf bag. Golf bags we didn't even bring with us since we weren't planning on playing that day. We just wanted some info.

He obtained about the same amount of information that I would have. In other words, not much. So we went to another golf course. This time it was a private golf course. We can't join the country club. But we can play golf at that course through the state golf association. We went to see the man who runs that deal to get the membership info. On our way into the facility, we had to dodge goats and dogs. We passed a compound that looked like it had been used as a prison in the past.

Back to golf...as foreigners, we can play for three years. That's it. At the end of three years, no more golf. So, if you're an expat golfer in Chennai, you'd better hope you won't be living here any more than 3 years or you'll have abrupt withdrawals. OK, so Golf Guy told us how much it would cost for our "one time fees", "membership fees", and "annual fees." These fees differed for all three of us. Let's face it, he was pulling these numbers out of the clear blue sky. I asked if he had a brochure with the printed fees so I could remember all the numbers he just told us. "Oh, the fees just changed," he told us, looking rather pleased with himself. Uh huh...like in the last 30 seconds, they did.

On our way back out, McGyver told us he found out what the compound was used for. It's where the military slaughters the goats and cows every Sunday. Haha. Welcome to golf in Chennai folks.

There's a monthly orientation that we must attend before we can play. We missed the one for October and will have to wait until November for the next one. Now that the rains have started, I'm wondering if we just wait a little longer.

(Note: We've been given the runaround and it doesn't look like we'll ever get to golf.)

Our housekeeper cum cook had been with us long past her expiration date. I wanted to replace her a long time ago. I felt guilty and couldn't fire her, even though she has ruined a lot of laundry and food along the way...not to mention she just annoyed me in general. It got to the point where we took over the cooking because we had been sick for so long. My friends, my family, even my parents urged me to fire her.

Part of the problem is that it's difficult for household staff to have any respect for valuable items. They don't care about our belongings the way we do. They don't own such things so it's a hard thing to teach. With cooking, they likely don't own refrigerators so they don't understand that uncooked meat must be kept in the fridge. Then they've had a lifetime to build up a resistance to whatever is in the water that makes us sick.

Yesterday I reached the limit, which is beyond my real limit, since I had reached my real limit a long time ago. She ruined a Longaberger table runner. She launched into one of her, "It's not my fault madam..." speeches and I just held up my hand and walked away. I didn't want to come unglued over one more ruined item so I went upstairs to cool down. Talk to the hand.

So, here's how my inner dialog went...

OK, so it's another ruined item.

Yeah, but it's retired Longaberger item.

But maybe you're placing too much emphasis on material things.

Maybe I am, but I've had a *lot* of ruined stuff lately. When do I draw the line?

But you can't fire her because she's the only source of income for her family.

If I were running a business, what would I do?

I would fire her. It's business, after all.

I gave her many chances and she was not teachable. Every time I tried, I got the, "I know madam." Mmmm, no. Apparently you don't.

I've tried to be fair about all of this. She's been with us a lot longer than she should have been.

Hmmmmmm.....

And what would I say? I tried to fire her on at least two other occasions and wimped out.

Just tell her it's not working out and today is her last day of work.

But I'll never find another housekeeper that can handle being around a golden retriever.

You just had new clothing made to replace your ruined clothing. One wash or ironing and it will all be ruined again.

Will I be able to handle all the housework in this big house?

Yeah, probably not. Maybe Kasturi could come in each morning to sweep.

Today's Friday, it's nearly the end of the month, I've waited too long as it is, it has to be today.

Maybe I can wait until Sir gets home.

Ohhhh, eeerrrrr.....Just do it Danie. You can do it. This is your house, your family. You can do this. *Sigh*

So I went downstairs close to 5pm. I knew she wouldn't be coming up to say goodbye as she usually did. I told her it wasn't working out and today would be her last day. Then it began, but madam this and but madam that. See, this was one of my big issues, she was unteachable. She was always right and never to blame. I told her to get her things, it was time to go. Half way to the door, she asked me to give her two weeks to find another job. Not unreasonable on the surface, but that's two weeks to clean us out.

Then, the oddest thing happened. She asked me for a bonus. Only in India would you fire someone and then they expect you to give them a bonus. Finally, I had to give her the hand again. There was nothing left to talk about it. I was done.

I spent the rest of the evening alternating between relief and guilt. I feel free, but I also feel overwhelmed at taking care of this massive house on my own. I feel guilty too. I don't like to end anyone's employment.

I'm not in a hurry to find another housekeeper...so you may want to leave your shoes on if you come to visit.

Photo Credit: Connor B.

Photo Credit: Connor B.

24 Hours of Rain

The rain has stopped. Temporarily, I'm sure. So, how did we make out with that much rain?

- School is canceled today.

- The streets surrounding our house were flooded, it was like having a moat.

- The air conditioners and windows leaked

- Our bathroom ceiling is leaking again. Water poured in through the living room wall. Yes, the wall!

- The rooftop terrace flooded with 4-5 inches of water.

- The backyard flooded with 4-5 inches of water. The sewage drains filled up (and overflowed?) and it smelled sooooo bad... even inside the house.

- The side of the swimming pool caved in.

...Otherwise, we did just fine!

Now that the rain has stopped, all of the water seems to have drained in our backyard and the streets. Can't wait to see what our landlords have to say about the pool though.

As we were going from room to room last night assessing our leaky house, I ventured into the closet in one of the guest rooms where winter coats and dresses are stored. Everything is covered in mildew. I don't know where else to store these things but it in the meantime, it will all need to be cleaned...*sigh*

Follow up Note: So, it turns out, there's more! The ground on the other side of the pool has also sunken in but there doesn't seem to be any damage to the pool on that side (so far). Connor went out to play soccer before it starts to rain again. The landlord came by and that's how we found out that the pump house for the pool has flooded too. Which makes complete sense because the water (in the photo) is not near the top of the pool. Last night, it was up to rim and about to overflow. I did wonder, this morning, where all that water went. Connor took some photos for me (since I'm so busy inside laundering wet towels and mopping floors).

Judging from the photos, the water looks to be almost 3 feet deep. Does anyone know how long monsoon lasts?

Happy Halloween

BOO!

Last night, we watched the latest episode of *Life is Wild*[1]. Connor really likes this show about a blended family that moves from New York City to Africa in hopes of family bonding. Lives of expats and all it entails--on TV!

On last night's episode, they were celebrating South African Heritage Day which coincided with Halloween. How these expats could plausibly decorate the house for Halloween when they arrived in South Africa with just a few suitcases is beyond me. Ahhhh, the magic of television.

Other than a table runner, we have not decorated for Halloween and we will not be handing out candy tonight. I started feeling guilty, especially after the massive effort I put into last year's Halloween/Birthday party bash. I wondered if Connor would be feeling sad for missing out.

It was a good reminder that while participating in some of the local customs, it's important to also participate in our own customs too and not abandon them just because we're expats. I'm off to see if I can at least make some cupcakes for tonight and put together a Halloween dinner of champions. I may even have to pull Princess Leia or Fiona out of storage.

Happy Halloween Y'all!

1 http://www.cwtv.com/shows/life-is-wild

Housework is a Four Letter Word

The landlord came back with four men in tow to look at the pool again. He ordered Kasturi to start bailing out the water from the pump house. Yeah. I don't think so. Since when did our staff become his laborers? AND, how about he stick his own two feet in that water and risk possible electrocution before he ask her to do it? I had The King up in my grill and JB had McGyver up in his about the whole thing. They were both very upset with the landlord, and understandably concerned for Kasturi. JB and I are on the same page, she's not doing it.

Speaking of The King...our staff either thinks I'm completely useless or they just can't comprehend madam doing housework. The King was inside today escorting the phone people and translating for me (yes, we're still trying to sort out the bad phone lines and internet). He told me that he and McGyver are "very cut up" that madam is doing housework. They're also worried that I won't go anywhere because I have housework to do. Yeah right. The housework can wait if I have an excuse to get out of the house!

I explained that I did the housework in the US. I didn't have a driver, a housekeeper, a cook, a sweeper, a gardener or guards. *I* did it. He just stared at me with a blank look, not knowing what to say to that. Hilarious! He said he could find me a cook and a good housekeeper. No really. I don't want either one. So far so good with Kasturi coming in to sweep each morning. I'm also going to have her take the trash down the street to the dumpster daily since the guards get cranky when I do it.

This morning as I was mopping up the rainwater and doing laundry, I realized how inefficient and out-of-practice I am at doing housework...and it's only been 6 months. I was going back and forth, back and forth, far more than I needed to. When JB got home, I realized how tough it's going to be to whip him and Connor back into the routine of doing chores, putting things away that they use and picking up after themselves. They're already begging me to hire someone. JB says he gives it a week before I have interviews scheduled. Hmph.

Funny moment...I'm also not sure how I managed to do it, but the clothes washer overflowed today. Bubbly water everywhere. I grabbed the mop, realized it smelled horrible and went about getting another one out of storage. I decided to try a different kind and the mop head broke off. I was almost done, so here I was, bent over, mopping up the water with the mop head in my hand. I must have looked hilarious.

It won't be long and this house will be running like a well-oiled machine.

Seriously.

Dogs and "gods" on Halloween

Halloween was a whopper.

I picked Connor up at school and on the way home he said he would like to get an eye mask to wear for the morning drives--like the kind that the airlines hand out on overnight flights. That morning, he saw a dog that had been killed. He said that it looked like there was an actual tire path through the center of the dog. Then he passed another dog that was trying to get up but it was so sick he could not stand. "How can people just walk by and not help the dogs? How come they don't care? What is wrong with people?" He wanted to know. He was very upset.

We had our Halloween dinner of vomit (mac and cheese with green food coloring for the putrid gray affect), worms (slivered hot dogs, a rare treat in India), ice cold blood (raspberry Crystal Light) and cupcakes. Which brings us to the dessert conversation...

Religion. Connor has a strong Christian faith and he is having a tough time accepting that Hindus pray to many "gods" and none of their "gods" have anything to do with Jesus.

So, humanity, animal cruelty, and faith were the heavy topics of the day. All this on the heals of our deep freeze failing and losing everything that was in it, as well as, the sewage contaminating our water tank.

Maybe another cupcake is needed in order to ponder it all.

Who is Michael Clayton?

When I asked my sister how her weekend was, she responded with, "We went to see Michael Clayton this weekend." The name didn't ring a bell. Was I supposed to know this person? Was he a mutual friend? My mind raced to put a face to the name but nothing was coming to me.

Apparently, Michael Clayton is the latest movie starring George Clooney. Who knew? I didn't! We are so behind on what's playing in the theaters. We consider ourselves lucky if we can find DVD's from the 80's that aren't so scratched that they'll still play. OK, that may be exaggerating a little bit, but not by much.

My point is, we are out of the movie loop. I have no idea what is playing in theaters or what trailers are getting everyone hyped up to head to the movies. Movies were a common topic of interest between me and my sister. It's weird to not be able to talk about something that I used to know about.

…and that is just *one* example of where I'm out of the loop.

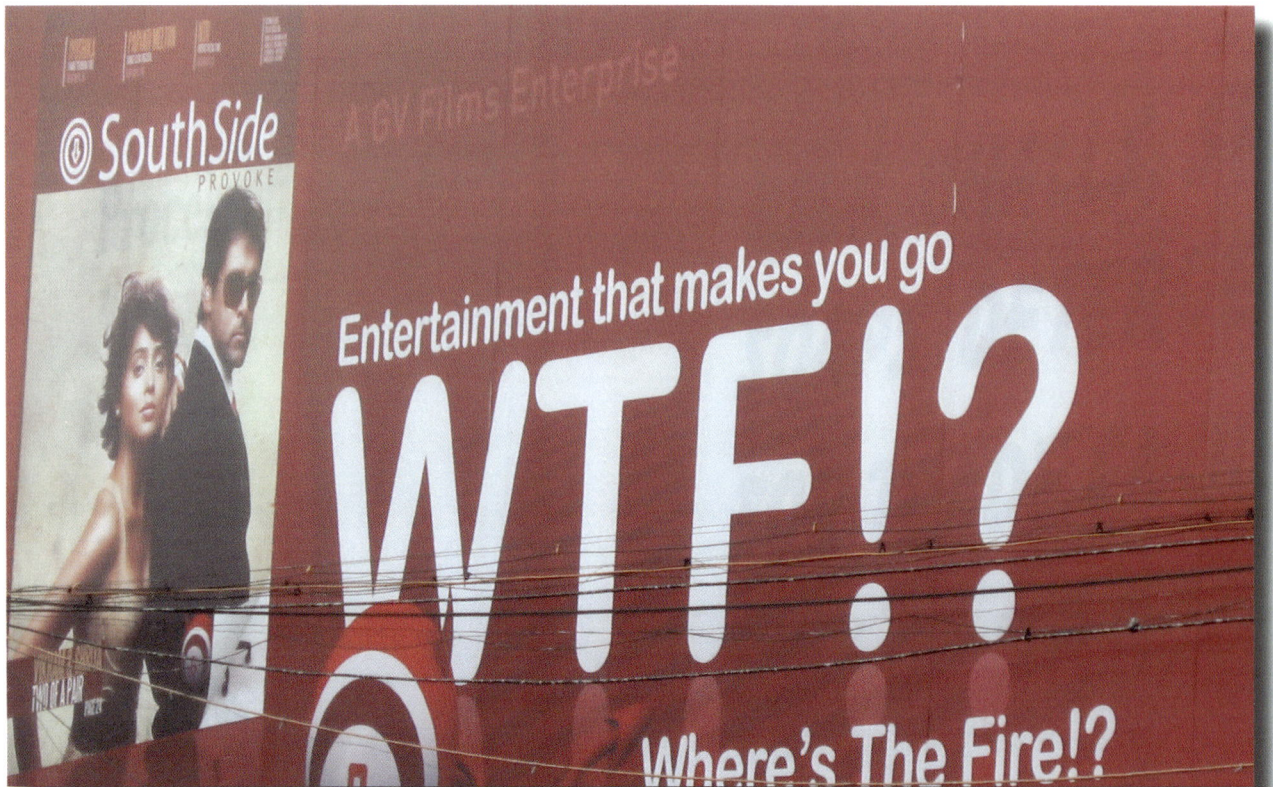

More Indian Advertisements

We drove by this sign the other night and laughed our butts off. McGyver totally didn't see the humor in it. He was puzzled when I told him I would need to get a photo the next time we drove by. On our way to the Park Hotel today, he said, "Madam, do you have camera? The sign." I fumbled to get my camera, and got the photo. "Is funny, madam?" We explained what "WTF?" stands for everywhere else. Yeah, he thought that was pretty funny. None of us could figure out what this was actually advertising, although McGyver says the guy with the glasses is a famous actor. I think he looks like a 'Boss' wannabe.

We finished off the last of the orange Tic Tacs today. No more until our next food shipment. McGyver likes them too. Shortly after we emptied the little container, we came across an ad for "Tit Bits" on the back of an auto rickshaw. We thought this was pretty funny too. Again, we explained why we thought it was funny to McGyver. I'm sure the man thinks we're nuts.

McGyver tells us that Tic Tacs/Tit Bits are new to India. So far, they're only available in mint flavor. Cost for the packages shown in the above photo are (approx US prices) .01, .03 and .25 for the little box (the same size as our boxes of Tic Tacs).

And last night, we drove past Wang's Kitchen. JB and I just looked at one another and cracked up. We didn't bother explaining that one.

We see STD signs for the phone, UTI signs for the bank and various other abbreviations that would make any North-American snicker.

Yeah, we're total juveniles but we get our kicks when we can.

Photo Credit: John B.

It was a big weekend. Well, I think it was. Nine months after moving here, we finally had a date (almost). Connor was attending the SAISA Swim Party so we went out for drinks and seafood. The party ended earlier than the invitation specified so Connor joined us just as our main course was being served. Almost a date.

I believe I've gotten to the point where I can focus on some of the things that I used to enjoy. I finally have enough attention span to start reading *The Space Between Us* by Thrity Umrigar. I also had enough focus to unpack our geocaching (prounounced "geocashing") backpack. And that's really what this post is about. Geocaching[1], what is it?

> Geocaching is an entertaining adventure game for gps users. Participating in a cache hunt is a good way to take advantage of the wonderful features and capability of a gps unit. The basic idea is to have individuals and organizations set up caches all over the world and share the locations of these caches on the internet. GPS users can then use the location coordinates to find the caches. Once found, a cache may provide the visitor with a wide variety of rewards. All the visitor is asked to do is if they get something they should try to leave something for the cache.
> - Groundspeak Geocaching FAQ[2]

Sounds easy huh? Not always. Sometimes the container blends in to its surroundings and is very difficult to find, or hard to get to. I like the geocaches that have a problem-solving element to it in order to obtain the coordinates. There are about a dozen different types of caches[3].

The really cool thing about this hobby for us is that there are caches around the entire globe. I plan to check a few caches when we go to Dubai this week (just two more days). And as I was planning our spring break trip to Egypt, I found lots of caches, including a mystery earth cache where the geocacher has to figure out the coordinates of the center of a specific pyramid. So cool. Yeah, I'm such a nerd.

There aren't many caches in this area of India. That number will be increasing, though, because we plan to hide a few. You would be surprised to know that there are likely many caches in your area. Check it out[4].

Two rules that are near and dear to geocachers are *Leave No Trace*[5] and *Cache in, Trash Out*[6]. Many geocachers combine this hobby with travel, photography or cross-training. We used to like picking up caches in city locations over lunch or after we were done with homeschool. After church on Sundays, we picked the ones that provided us with a nature walk so Kramer could come with us. Surprisingly, Kramer has sniffed out a few caches for us when we've been stumped. It was a great way to keep Connor and I busy on the Saturdays that JB had his EMBA program.

I've really missed it and I'm looking forward to finding at least one cache whenever we travel. If you decide to give it a try, keep an eye out for us, we're Team Maple Leaf[7].

[1] http://www.geocaching.com/

[2] http://www.geocaching.com/faq/

[3] http://www.geocaching.com/about/cache_types.aspx

[4] http://www.geocaching.com/seek/gmnearest.aspx?lat=44.402391829093915&lng=-96.416015625&zm=4&mt=m

[5] http://www.lnt.org/

[6] http://www.cacheintrashout.org/

[7] http://www.geocaching.com/profile/Default.aspx?guid=dcc60114-2ebc-45b5-8803-239fd09363b1

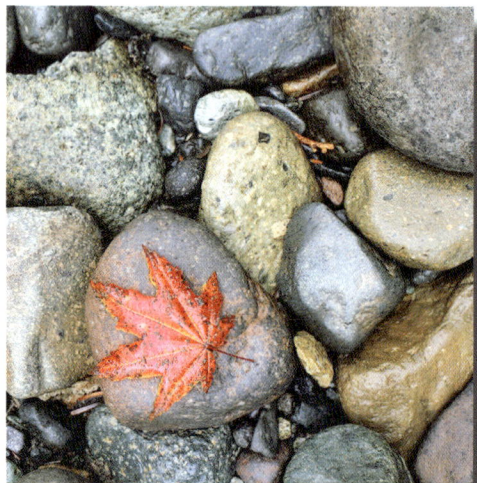

I went geocaching this morning. I went to St. Thomas' Mount to retrieve a travel coin which I will drop off at another cache in Dubai later this week.

Geocaching is more challenging when having to tell a driver how to get there--and not being sure in the first place! I explained what I was going to do but I think he thought I was crazy. We got to the park and it was very overgrown. McGyver was worried about snakes so he decided to come with me. Ok, he's soooo hooked. Give a guy a little handheld GPS receiver that beeps and has buttons--it doesn't matter what nationality they are--soooo hooked. Sometimes when a cache is hidden in an area where there are a lot of non-cachers (aka muggles), one needs to be a little bit stealthy so the cache doesn't get found out (and stolen). Like it's not hard enough to blend in when you're the only white person around for miles, but the white uniform in tow is hardly low-key.

So one of the goals of geocachers is to leave the location a little better than you found it. That means *Cache In, Trash Out*. McGyver definitely thought I was crazy to be picking up trash as we walked back to the car.

But he is sooooo hooked.

It was a pleasant four hour flight from Chennai to Dubai. Ever since our arrival, my thoughts have been in terms of blog posts...somewhat how I used to think in terms of scrapbook layouts. As I was running through my blog post thoughts, I noticed my thoughts were fast and erratic. The truth is, I'm pretty sure I lack the basic talent necessary to describe this whole experience in words to do it the justice it deserves.

The foreigner to Arab ratio here is about 50-50. That means, as strange as we are, we're not getting sideway glances. I never thought I would find my "normal" in the middle east. I'm overwhelmed.

As we were landing, we could see sand. Sand that went on for as far as we could see. It was my first view of a desert. Growing up on the ocean, I thought I would hate it. After living in a very crowded city where "personal space" is an unknown concept, the desert looks magnificent.

The Dubai airport is like nothing I've ever seen before. Massive palm trees, Rolex clocks on the walls, modern shops and restaurants. I'm not kidding when I say I could have just stayed at the airport for four days and been happy as a clam. But it got better.

Our driver was from Chennai. Ironic, no? He felt the need to explain the differences between the two cities, which is pretty funny, because it's as obvious as night and day. Big beautiful multi-lane highways with left-hand drive cars. No autorickshaws, over-crowded buses or livestock. We could have easily driven ourselves. What a thought! As we drove from airport to hotel, our excitement escalated as we saw restaurants, stores and brands we could identify with. Every building looks like a work of modern art and a defiance of engineering...and budget. Even something you would think would be very common, like Bridgestone Tires, is in a building worthy of an award. For a former architecture student--sweet.

The Kempinski Hotel is...well, words like awesome, incredible and amazing are meaningless...boring. Even the elevators with troughs built into the walls for pot-pourri are over the top. The bathrooms...I considered a four-day bathing marathon. I'm sure I'll bathe at least twice a day, because I can. And I'll do it in an unlimited supply of hot, odorless water. The water from the tap...it's drinkable! The vegetables...edible!

The Mall of the Emirates. In one word, no, make it two...scratch that...three...Danie's Personal Nirvana. I'm not a flashy dresser. I'm not a "fashionable" person. I dress very conservatively. Simple, barely-there, makeup. The women here are *stylin'*. I considered heavying up on the eyeliner to blend in, but on me it wouldn't look exotic at all, I'd look like a 'ho'. I'll stick with my plain janeness but this mall will exceed satisfying my every fetish and whim for jewelry, hand bags and shoes (in that order). It will more than satisfy our need for distraction, entertainment and amusement. And with the list of American and familiar restaurants and kiosks, and, and, and, and, and, we may not even try to local food this time around. It may not be quite as big West Edmonton Mall but the shops here get my *wow*.

Ski Dubai. We saw it on *Extreme Engineering* and dreamed of going there. Oh my, we're actually here. One step outside our hotel into the mall and we see the bottom of the ski slopes. I'm so excited to be here. I'm so excited to see Connor in this environment, even he can't be blasé in his nearly-11-traveled-around-the-world-coolness. His freak-flag is flying high!

So, what did we do on our first night in Dubai? We went to McDonalds (of course). I hazard to say that the food was better than in the US, or maybe it's just because we hadn't had it in so long that it was just so good. No funky spice. Yum yum. We walked around the mall in a daze, just soaking it all in...Borders Book Store (Mega magazine rack and English books), Virgin Megastore (the latest books, CDs, DVDs and electronics), Starbucks (caramel frappaccino...it keeps getting better and better), a bath and soft, fluffy, luxurious bedding.

I've got my work cut out. I'm not sure if four days will be enough

Ski Dubai

Ski Dubai[1] described by Connor..."awesome" and "so cool!" Yeah. That's a pretty fair assessment.

We arrived in the evening just as it was getting dark. The center strip of Ski Dubai was lit up with alternating colors.

So, Connor actually didn't want to go skiing. He did, but he didn't. He was five years old the last time he skied. He was nervous. The good thing about Ski Dubai is that it's geared toward new or non-skiers.

Upon arrival, we were each given a ski jacket, snow pants, boots, skis, and a helmet for Connor. We used our own hats and mittens but it was only -3C with no wind so it wasn't cold (by Canadian standards...the Arabians were freezing). We paid for two hours of skiing. Lessons were available for skiing and snowboarding but we skipped that part. I took Connor to the "bunny slope" for a little practice. I remember when I first learned to ski at the age of 7. Mastering the t-bar lift is no easy feat for a) a kid and b) a new skier. Ski Dubai cleverly uses conveyor ramps...just stand on it. We did that a few times giving Connor a chance to get the hang of maneuvering the cones on the slope, then he graduated to the chair lift. By the end of the two hours, he was going to the very top of the hill.

There were professional photographers throughout. We picked out two for souvenirs. I showed them to McGyver and he just can't comprehend it. "Snow? In a building? Skiing? In the desert? And it's at the shopping mall, madam?" It's almost as good as seeing the joy on your child's face when they experience something new. What fun.

[1] http://www.skidxb.com/English/default.aspx

Dubai: The Last Day

How did we spend our last few hours in Dubai? By going to the most massive grocery store I've ever seen. I can't even say that it's like the US because it was better. Yes, better. We were so overwhelmed, we couldn't even decide what to bring back to India with us. I really wish I could've stuffed my suitcase with meat (imported from 6 different countries) or produce (I just wanted to sit down and start eating it fresh). The variety was stunning.

That tiny little figure with the white shirt, looking confused, that's JB. And that was just the cookie aisle, folks. McGyver said it looks like an airport. That aisle is about as wide as our bedroom!

Maybe you shop at a place like this all time and can't comprehend our excitement. For the fun of contrast, here's where we shop in Chennai...

I do have to admit that since their massive renovation, it's improved quite a bit. I wish I had taken photos before they expanded. We're lucky to have Amma Naana as they do offer a nice variety of imported (price gouged) goods when they're not sold out. Like, $22 USD for a bottle of imported Kraft Parmesan Cheese, for example.

So, what did we buy at the Carrefour grocery store in Dubai? Mostly breads. Some packages of soup, we each picked a bag of chippies (they even had my very favorite...sea salt and cracked black pepper), a few party bag items for Connor's birthday, icing sugar, magazines, along with a few health & beauty items. We also brought back some Starbucks coffee for a friend.

Carrefour also included a huge home department, clothing department, electronics department, and, and, and...it was fun and exciting, sad and depressing, all at the same time.

Dubai and Back

We're back in Chennai after a lovely trip to Dubai (pronounced Do-Buy for good reason). It was like a trip to Disneyland.

The hotel was heaven. The mall, superb. The food...well, I ate big delicious salads every day. A ceasar salad with garlic lime shrimp, a road-house salad, a nicoise salad and a quesadilla explosion salad. I've really missed salads. It was so nice to eat vegetables, have ice in our drinks and brush our teeth with tap water. It was also beyond nice to have a bath everyday in water that didn't have a foul odor. Excellent water pressure that filled the tub in about 3 minutes (instead of 25).

I would like to tell you that we tore up Dubai seeing and doing everything that was offered, but the truth is, we never left the hotel/mall. By the end of the first day, my feet were blistered and I bought some running shoes to get me through. We hung out at the pool, went to the gym, strolled through the mall everyday and ate at the terrific variety of restaurants. We skied. We celebrated Connor's birthday at Magic Planet. We were supposed to go to a geocaching event but missed it so I could knock off a few more things on my list of to-dos. We packed our clothes into small suitcases and put those into bigger empty suitcases...glad we did.

Why didn't I blog about Dubai while I was in Dubai? Well, the main reason is that I couldn't process it all. I probably still can't. Connor couldn't either. That's why his blog posts[1] mainly consisted of "awesome" and "so cool." Secondly, some of the websites and services that I use to maintain this blog were inaccessible from Dubai. For example, the Meez website[2] gave this error:

> Blocked ...the site you are attempting to visit has been blocked due to its content being inconsistent with the religious, cultural, political and moral values of the United Arab Emirates. If you think this site should not be blocked, please visit the feedback forum on our website blah blah blah...

The people were very friendly. It was soooo clean. We noticed a very different work ethic and attitude. And I haven't even told you about our trip through the grocery store...major culture shock there. This trip certainly gave us a glimpse that repatriation is going to be tough. But not nearly as tough as it was coming back to Chennai.

I don't understand how a society can be so dysfunctional. JB says I shouldn't dignify it with a blog post. In a way, he's right, but this is my therapy so here it goes.... As we were all standing to get off the aircraft, a man barreled his way down the aisle and literally threw Connor into a seat so he could get ahead. Of a child!! Have you ever been so mad that you can literally feel the physical change in your body? A couple of flights landed at the airport at the same time last night. Immigration was a nightmare. I'm pretty sure that Chennai airport is the only airport in the world that doesn't have a "coral queue." The kind of queue that forces everyone to wait their turn for the next available immigration officer. Oh no, Chennai is a bloody free for all of rudeness. When it was all said and done, after 600 people cut in line and we were endlessly shoved around, we were the last people to clear immigration. Oh yeah. The other officers were pouring their tea while we were finishing up! When we finally got to baggage claim, an Indian woman came over to me and told me she was embarrassed to be Indian and what must foreigners think when they arrive in Chennai? I was so angry and so tired and so wasn't capable of having a polite conversation, all I could say was, "Don't get me started. Please, don't get me started." I was so scared I was going to say something mean, I just couldn't even talk to her. She was a nice lady too, I had chatted with her at the airport in Dubai. The whole experience was truly appalling. We arrived home exhausted, angry and so dismayed to have to be back here.

It was a pleasure to be greeted by familiar smiling faces when we exited the airport. McGyver's first question...did we go geocaching? He's sooo hooked. Because of the Diwali celebrations, he stayed at the house with Kramer for two nights. Kramer is petrified of the firecrackers. He comes completely unhinged, trying to climb into my lap, whimpering and shaking. If he hears them while he's in the car, he tries to climb into McGyver's lap while he's driving. One of those nights, the firecrackers were so bad that McGyver told us he took Kramer for a drive to the beach and they hung out in the car with the air conditioning running for two hours. Before we left for Dubai, I made up the guestroom for McGyver. He insisted that he would sleep on the floor in the hallway with the dog. I objected very strongly. Kramer doesn't even sleep on the floor! JB had to insist that McGyver use the guestroom. He did, and Kramer slept with him. While I was away, he also bathed Kramer and mopped the floors because he said he didn't want me to have to do it when I got back. That's our McGyver.

So, it will take a few days to readjust back to the real world...I'm sure I'll be fighting it every step of the way.

[1] http://heheelys.blogspot.com/2007/11/whoa.html

[2] http://www.meez.com/home.dm?refname=earthtodanie

International Geocaching

We had one geocache to check out while we were in Dubai. I didn't want to spend a lot of time on it, so I checked the spoiler photos. I'm glad I did because it was hard to find even with spoilers in mind. We dropped off a travel coin in a stairwell of the shopping mall (before it was open for business). Here's the thing though, I am *so* lucky that I wasn't arrested for using a GPSr in Dubai! It never even occurred to me that it might be an issue.

> Taking photographs of potentially-sensitive UAE military and civilian sites, or foreign diplomatic missions, including the U.S. Embassy, may result in arrest, detention and/or prosecution by local authorities. In addition, engaging in mapping activities, especially mapping which includes the use of GPS equipment, without coordination with UAE authorities, may have the same consequences. - U.S. State Department website

How easy would it have been for someone to see me walking around the Mall of the Emirates parking lot with my GPSr and think I was doing something fishy? Lesson learned. From now on, I'm going to check every country study before I travel to that area.

I'm not over the not-so-hilarious image of me in a middle eastern prison cell. I wonder if the prison cells are on par with the luxury of everything else in Dubai.

I'd prefer not to find out first hand. Besides, I doubt I could create an avatar for that.

Character Building

I always thought that expats who say they love living in India are big liars. I have a Canadian friend here who says, "You have to be called to India in order to love it."

Yesterday, I was chatting with someone who is gearing up to leave India. In that conversation she said that living in India reveals your true character. I don't think I heard anything else after that. JB and I talked about it last night and again this morning. She's spot on. Living in India does reveal your true character. And that might be a tough pill to swallow for me. I'm not sure I like what living in India is revealing to me about my character, but there it is staring me in the face and giving me the opportunity to deal with it.

One thing I've learned about myself since we've lived here is that I'm not as emotionally, mentally or physically strong as I thought I was. And that by no means indicates that I'm on the verge of a nervous breakdown because I'm still very strong in those areas. I'm just not the powerhouse I thought I was, which really makes me mad. Perhaps this will be an evolving thing that will require more time.

I'm not in a hurry to adjust to living in India. I've got time. I don't care if I ever adjust to India. I don't want there to come a day when I've adjusted to the things I see here every day. It doesn't mean that that I'm not doing well. It doesn't mean that I'm unhappy. It means I'm building character. And I'm looking forward to learning and growing along the way...as painful as that may be at times.

Photo Credit: John B.

◥ School Zone Photo

Um. Er. Uhhhh. Mmm. Yeah, I got nothing.

◥ Rate of Inflation

The rate of inflation in Chennai is staggering. House and apartment rental prices are skyrocketing. It's becoming impossible to find decent (by north American standards) housing without paying a fortune. And because the big companies are paying big rent, the rent keeps increasing. So expats who aren't here with big companies can't find decent affordable housing...and that's if the landlord will even rent to them without the support of a multi-national company behind them. There was a shop that some expat friends were enjoying. They last time they went in, the prices had nearly doubled. I've heard that a local expat magazine will be doing an article on this shop which means the prices will likely go up yet again.

I went to lunch with a friend this week. Upon arrival, she ordered a cappuccino. She ordered a second cappuccino with dessert (we were such moos). Two cappuccinos, two different prices. I thought it was just an error on the bill so I showed it to the waiter. He got the boss who told us he had just changed the price in the system during the time we were having lunch. "No problem madame, I fix right away." He fixed the bill alright! He increased the price of the first cappuccino instead of lowering the price of the second cappuccino.

...One more instance where I should have kept my big mouth shut. One more example of "customer service" in India.

Photo Credit: John B

Bloggers Meet at Photo Competition

We attended Global Adjustments[1] 10th Annual Expat Photo Competition award ceremony and brunch last Sunday. Expats who submitted photos were asked to arrive early. We arrived too early so we went to the coffee shop in the lobby for a coffee and a pre-brunch snack. Glad we did because by the time brunch was served my tummy was rumbling! While we were sitting there, a lady walks out of the book shop and we recognize one another instantly. Comical considering we'd never met. I've been reading Nancy's blog[2] ever since the time I knew I would be moving to India. She wished Connor a happy birthday and the look on his face was priceless…how did she know? As it turns out, she reads my blog too.

I went into the ballroom and sat in my assigned seat. I felt silly sitting alone in the first row. Then Basia came along. I've been reading Basia's blog[3] for a long time too, and I love her photographs. After reading about their adventures, I knew I would really like these women if I ever met them. After the award ceremony, JB and Connor came to my seat and we made introductions. JB said, "Oh, this is the lady that drank cow's blood in Africa." Basia wished Connor a happy birthday, and again, he looked so confused. I told him that this is the lady whose blog we read, "You know, the one that had a photo of the monkey with blue testicles." Immediate recognition! He really loved those monkeys.

Meeting these two women made my day. They're far more adventurous than I am…and much better photographers! I see a different India/world through their blogs.

Global Adjustments put on a stage show reflecting the Expat Life Cycle. It was fun to see expats that I knew from school dancing to Indian music. They did a fantastic job, especially considering the small amount of time they had to practice.

Like frosting on the cake, I placed Second for one of the photos I entered of Coconut Guy.

[1] http://globaladjustments.com   [2] http://nmj3.blogspot.com/   [3] http://basia.blog-city.com/

You Light Up My Life

Saturday night was another Hindu festival. I don't think I ever got a straight answer on what it was really about. One minute it was about Shiva and blessing married couples. The next minute, it was about rain and if it didn't rain to put out the oil lamps on a mountain somewhere, then there would be a great famine. Lots of statistics were cited by The King about the last famine and dead chief ministers and no rice. It was all very confusing and I probably should be taking notes when he tells me stuff.

This was McGyver's doing with the help of The King. They did a good job and it looked really pretty. It was a complete surprise to us. We were inside watching a movie. They called us to come outside. They had placed lit oil lamps around the entrances, the pool, the front gate and on the roof of the carports. We went out into the street and our neighbors had oil lamps lit as well.

McGyver and The King, they light up my life.

You're Hired

I received an email last week about a US family who was leaving Chennai and looking for someone to hire their staff. The email was about a dobi who came highly recommended. I know, what's a dobi, right? I had no idea. A dobi is a person who provides laundry services. And considering how far behind I am on ironing-- "Honey, which shirt do you want to wear tomorrow so I can iron it before I go to bed?"--JB said, "Hire him." So, although it wasn't a package deal, this family also had a housekeeper who was also needing a new job.

I've done alright doing it all on my own. I haven't even minded it. I'm not a fan of having that many people around, so I have them staggered. Dobi Guy will come twice per week and Priya will come three times per week. Dobi Guy didn't even look daunted when I showed him my backlog of ironing. He laughed when I told him he didn't have to iron my sheets. I've never ironed my own sheets, I never will iron my sheets and I don't expect him to do something I'm not going to do myself. He said he would fold them in such a way there would be no creases. Seriously, I can sleep on creased sheets. I've been doing it my whole life.

Both Priya (the housekeeper) and Kannan (Dobi Guy) speak little English. I had The King in here this morning explaining life with Kramer in Tamil after I found Kramer chewing on Priya's flip flop, then with 2 socks in his mouth, then chowing down on a sheet of Bounce. First things first, train new staff to not kill dog.

Priya is young. She has a very pleasant demeanor and is doing a good job. I'm pretty sure her last family didn't have a dishwasher. That was apparent after she washed the dishes by hand and organized them nicely into the dishwasher for storage. I guess a little more explanation is needed there. Perhaps in Tamil the second time around.

Kasturi (the sweeper) thought she was losing her indoor-gig with the arrival of a new housekeeper and thought she'd be getting a paycut (which I had no intention of doing) so apparently she was very upset with me. We got it sorted though and everyone is very happy with the arrangement. The gardener, who currently travels 3 hours each way to come to work is being evicted from the room he rents. He's moving into the servant quarters behind our house. And, we're doing something that I swore I wouldn't do, we're taking on the tuition payments for The King's son to finish up his last year of university. What does college cost in India? Approximately $25.00 USD per month.

A few weeks ago, someone told me that because the poor in North America will always have shelter and education, they'll always have hope. Giving someone a job, a place to live or an education doesn't seem like much, but in India, it's landing on the other side of hope.

Christmas Traditions

About a week until Home Leave and Christmas is starting to feel real. It's been difficult to get into the Christmas spirit here. Only 2.5% of people in India are Christian. Many Hindus celebrate Christmas for the lights, trees and presents. And there's something about "walking in a winter wonderland" in India that is down right depressing.

Today, with Christmas music blaring, I've set up our Nativity. Now I feel Christmas coming on.

Traditionally, we travel every other Christmas. We've lived in warmer climates or really far from "home" for a long time. Schlepping to Canada is no easy feat what with needing winter gear, which wasn't always available or feasible to purchase. So, Christmas, like wherever we live, has been whatever we make of it.

One year, we bought a 2' Christmas tree and decorated it with whatever we could find from a convenience store (mainly tin foil) while we were skiing in France with friends. Another year, we sat on the beach in the Bahamas, glad to feel the warmth of sand instead of cold snow. A few times, we've been blessed to have family accept our invitations to visit us for Christmas. My sister joined us in New Hampshire, and both of my sisters came to Illinois our first Christmas back from England (and I still have the framed photo of all of us in our matching jammies). One year, my dad came to North Carolina. And last year, JB's dad trekked to Illinois.

Along the way, we've started our own family traditions and have built upon the traditions of childhood Christmases.

I wonder which traditions Connor will keep.

Locked and Stocked!

My friend, Penny, is moving to Beijing in January. Our last two food shipments, she has...stocked...us...up. That ought to hold us over for a while since our shopper is leaving Illinois. Priya helped me organize the pantry, which is the upstairs kitchen sans cabinets/appliances. We keep the door closed with the air conditioning cranked to deter pesties.

The bulk of our shipments consist of lunch foods/snacks, canned veggies/soups, toiletries, cleaning supplies, good soda and dog food.

I'll be very disappointed when our food shipments get canceled.

She Scores!

I did a half hour of power shopping this morning and scored big.

I found two pair of shoes rather easily at the mall (miraculous to be sure), not even the power blackouts deterred me. When I went to a department store to find a handbag to match said shoes, the security guard wanted me to check the bag. As in, hand over to him for safekeeping while I shop. Ok, girls, you know what I'm talking about here...how does one match up bag to shoes if the shoes are checked in a cubby at the entrance two floors below? I tried to convey this logic to the security guard, who then snagged a random passerby for translation. Still no luck though. I had to move past logic on to plan B. I opened the bag, stuck my hand into one shoe box, then the other, pulling out one shoe from each box. The security guard said, "No." To which I politely answered, "Yes." After a little back-and-forth with Stranger Guy still looking on, I won.

And after I won the game, I continued to score. Off I went to find a handbag with two mismatched shoes crammed into my purse.

I feel like I've accomplished a lot. And the day is still young.

It's Time For Home Leave When...

...Your son suggests that you sprinkle cumin on the Thanksgiving Day turkey.

...You go to dinner and every word to the waiter from your kid is spoken with a Tamil accent.

...Your child amazes the staff with his ability to sing songs in Tamil and Hindi.

...Same child wants to download Indian Rockers from iTunes.

...Your dog obeys the staff...who don't speak English to him.

...Back to the kid...he knows all the Indian gods by name.

...Company's cafeteria food is yummy?

...It's mid-80's and you think it's too cold for air conditioning.

...Nuh-uh, way too cold to go swimming!

...You're on the edge of agreeing to wear a saree.

Quick! Board that flight!

Don't Let Political Correctness Make Christmas Obsolete

We're on Home Leave and since I finally have access to a real computer (instead of just my PDA), I jumped at the chance at free therapy by means of blogging. No kidding, this has been on my mind for several days and I can't stop thinking about it. Then again, I am a little OCD that way. I hadn't intended to write until I got back from Home Leave but this is a blogging 911.

So the journey from India to Canada, door-to-door, took 36 hours. That was a lot of time to ponder, watch movies, eat and sleep. Mostly ponder though, as I do.

The day that we left Chennai, JB walked through the factory and about 60 people wished him a Merry Christmas. Or, as they say, Happy Christmas. We've received cards and gifts from many non-Christmas-celebrating people. We're talking about Indian Hindus.

As we journeyed through the Dubai airport, we were in awe of the Christmas decorations. It was so beautiful. When we were there in November, several people had wished us a Merry Christmas. We're talking about Middle Eastern Muslims. If it was like this in Dubai, can you imagine what it will be like when we get to New York? We couldn't wait.

We anticipated the feelings of 'Home' and 'Christmas' to come over us when we reached JFK airport in New York. Wow. Were we disappointed. We expected Christmas decorations and a Christmassy feeling. Not one Christmas tree. We're talking about Americans. In a primarily Christian country. Nobody wished us a Merry Christmas. But one or two people did say, "Happy holidays." How politically correct.

So here's what I want to know...What the heck is our problem? We're so concerned about being "politically correct" that we've become anti-Christmas. We can't wish anyone a Merry Christmas in America. We can't decorate public places for Christmas. Oh no, it just might offend someone. Now, we go out of our way to ensure there are Hanukkah and Kwanzaa songs in the "winter program" in schools to show how politically correct we are. But we can't have any songs about the birth of Christ or the celebration of His birthday. That's not politically correct. That's anti-Christmas. So let's just call it what it is.

I've got to tell you, in case you're missing the tone here, I'm beyond appalled. I resent America placing a big fat censorship on Christmas. This is supposed to be a place that represents the freedom of speech and the freedom of religion. There is no freedom of Christmas. This is not the America that I love. I have every respect for other cultures and faiths. We can have it all. I wonder what Hindus in Asia and Muslims in the Middle East would think if they knew the controversy over Christmas in America.

According to Wikipedia, Political Correctness is defined as:

> Political correctness (adjectivally politically correct, both forms commonly abbreviated to PC) is a term used to describe language, ideas, policies, or behavior seen as seeking to minimize offence to racial, cultural, or other identity groups. Conversely, the term politically incorrect is used to refer to language or ideas that may cause offense or that are unconstrained by orthodoxy.

Well, guess what? My Canadian culture and my Christian identity group is highly offended. Disgustingly offended. In the process of being politically correct, we've offended Christians. *Big* time. And what are we going to do about *that*, In-One-God-We-Trust-America?

Stepping off my soap box now.

Merry Christmas everyone!

◤ Things I Miss About India

Happy New Year from Illinois! It's *very* cold here today and quite frankly, I'm ready to head back to India to thaw my toes. Here's what else I miss...

- Kramer.
- My bed.
- Expat friends.
- Our staff.
- Warmth.
- Routine.
- Flip-flops.
- Danie time.

Being my first trip back to the US, it's been really nice to reflect on our life in India while not being in India. It snaps everything back into perspective and has given me some clarity on what my goals will be for 2008.

So here's wishing you and yours a great 2008!

◤ Hilights of Home Leave

- Spending Christmas with my family, especially seeing my grandparents every day.
- Tim Horton's almost every morning for breakfast in Canada. Panera Bread every morning for breakfast in the US.
- Sling box is set up and ready to go.
- Snow.
- Geocaching in the snow.
- Meeting up with friends. Especially the two days we were able to spend with friends before they moved to China.
- Cow. Good eats.
- Home cooked meals.
- Christmas sweeties.
- Learning how to play Nertzy (also known as Nerts, Nerf, Gluck, Peanuts, Pounce, Solitaire Frenzy, Squeal, Squeak, Squid, Speed, Squinch, Racing Demon, Race Horse Rummy, Lucky Thirty, Grouch and Hallelujah). It is an extremely fast paced version of Solitaire, with multiple players each having a separate deck of cards. We're hooked!
- We really enjoyed watching American football on TV.
- Wii. And Guitar Hero. Even the grandparents played Wii!
- Haircuts. The Sri Lankan massacre has been salvaged.
- Attending a service at our home church in Peoria.
- Grocery shopping.
- Having a babysitter and stealing away on a date.
- Bulls game & game food. Bulls won by 1 point in the last 3 seconds of the game. What fun!

◤ Welcome Home

Had I known on Monday morning in Chicago that I would be wearing the same clothes for 4 days, I was going to say that I would have dressed more comfortably, but I would have stashed clean socks and underwear for the entire family in my handbag. And dressed more comfortably. By the time we arrived at the lounge in Dubai, I was nearly delirious over how funny our stinky, wrinkled little selves looked next to how coiffed and 'put-together' the other travelers were. We looked a frightful mess. Tired. And had worn the same socks for 4 days...ACK.

India to Nova Scotia (door-to-door) was 36 hours. Chicago to India (door-to-door) took about 60 hours.

I was so happy to be home. McGyver took Kramer to the airport to greet us (along with all the usual suspects) since we sent him a message saying there was going to be no luggage. Yeah, we're still working on that one. Currently, nobody can say for sure where our bags are. So, I guess the President owes us a shopping spree since it's his fault our flights were canceled, thereby losing our luggage.

When we arrived at the house, the staff seemed very happy to see us. I think they missed us. Actually, I missed them too.

There's a big blue star hanging from the guardhouse that lights up at night. They told us that since we weren't here to celebrate Christmas, they celebrated for us.

Kasturi decorated all the entrances with Kolams and flower petals to welcome us home. Priya gave me roses. Very sweet indeed. And they all had plenty of stories and reports.

It's good to be home.

Happy Pongal!

When I woke up on Sunday morning I didn't know that we would be celebrating Pongal. Just before we were heading out to brunch, The King rang to tell us that Priya (our housekeeper) had arrived with her brother and cousins to do some decorating. Hmmm, what kind of decorating? We became so fascinated that we hung out with them for the rest of the day, skipping brunch altogether. We didn't know that Priya was coming to the house on Sunday. She usually works M, W, F. I think it speaks volumes about her character that she wanted to come to decorate Kolams for us. They were very well prepared with several designs drawn on paper. They brought a dozen or so bags of rock salt and colored powders.

Kramer came out for a visit but the two boys were very scared of him, then he ran off with a bag of the colored powder in his mouth. He stayed inside (whining) most of the day. In the afternoon we brought him out on a leash. By the end of the day, everyone was loving on him and even kissing him.

I chose the design for the front door. I really wanted to try my own hand at Kolams but was told that you don't do your own. Someone does it for you and you do it for someone else.

The King told me that they had planned to have a boiling pot and rice, which is typical of the Pongal celebrations but they didn't think I'd want the mess. Oh yes, I want the mess. They can do anything they like! So off McGyver went to get sugar cane and a clay pot. Pool Guy stuck around for the festivities too.

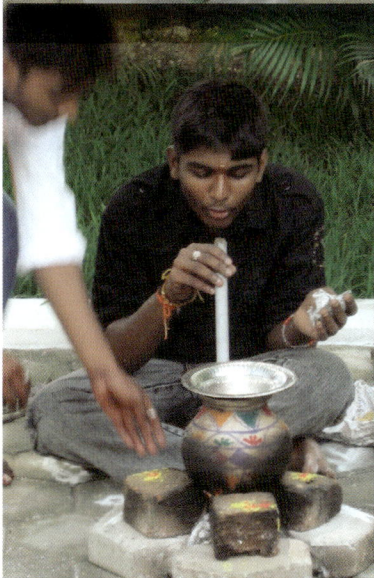

We all tried the sweet rice. It was the consistency of oatmeal, but sweeter. The four teens danced around the pot when it began to boil over.

And then, we hijacked Pongal. But that's a story for another day.

Today, there is a smoky blue fog and I can barely see the street outside our gate. Old linens, furniture and whatever else people would like to rid themselves of are being burned throughout the state of Tamil Nadu. JB said there were times on his way to work that he couldn't even see the side of the road.

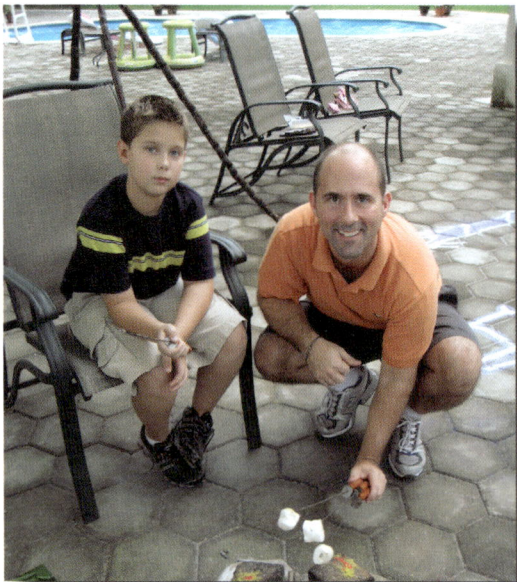

Pongal...Hijacked!

OK, so we Americanized Pongal a little bit. We invited some new friends over to experience the Pongal celebration with us. JB suggested that we bring out some snacks and drinks for everyone. Good idea! We noshed on Cheesy Chex Mix, Mixed Nuts and Raisinettes. The snacks were a hit. So were the Cherry flavored Pepsis and 7-Ups...none of which are available here.

We had all tried the Pongal rice and before the fire was put out Connor asked if he could roast some marshmallows. Absolutely! And knowing how what sweet-tooths Indians are, we figured they would really enjoy it. Then I had remembered that I had ordered supplies to make S'mores in a previous food shipment. We told McGyver about s'mores and when he translated to the teens, the looks on their faces relayed their horror.

McGyver really liked the marshmallows. He asked what they were made of and I told him it was pure sugar. "Yes, I like very much," he said. We made s'mores for everyone and they all seemed to enjoy it once they tried it. After everyone had left, I noticed Kramer chewing on what I thought was a napkin. When I opened his mouth to take the napkin out, he was gumming up a s'mores that someone threw around the corner...how many chews, mom? So at least one person didn't care for s'mores. Lucky Kramer.

Connor made another terrific suggestion. We should invite everyone upstairs to see the photos that we took throughout the day. People here love to see themselves in photos. It was a great idea and everyone really enjoyed seeing themselves projected onto the big screen. With lots of laughter, we all had fun.

Our good feelings about Pongal and Priya's kindness were also hijacked the following day. Before Priya and her friends left, we had given them a thank you note with some cash in it. We didn't want them to have to incur the cost of our Pongal celebrations so we wanted to give them a little money to help out. The next day, before Priya left work she asked me for money for the salt and colored powders. I understood the request and came to realize that we had given her 16 times the amount of money that was needed to cover her costs (to share with her friends). I couldn't communicate my lack of understanding as to the why. I called The King in to translate. Although we had given her plenty of money to cover her costs, she was asking for more. I was so disappointed. We thought she had been thoughtful and kind. We had enjoyed the day so much.

Later, I found out that The King and McGyver took turns yelling at her for trying to take advantage of us, finally telling her to get out. Although I made my disappointment known as kindly as I could, they were down right upset with her. I have no idea if she's planning to come back to work on Friday or not.

Last night when we arrived at home after dining out, there was a group of women in front of our gate. Kasturi and her friends were creating more Pongal Kolams. To which JB said, "I'm Pongaled out."

I'm by no means an expert but through a bit of experience I've found a pretty good system that works for me.

Luggage - Here's my theory on luggage--never buy *black* luggage. Too many people have black luggage and your bag is too easily mistaken for someone else's. Never use designer luggage. If a bag is going to get stolen off the conveyor belt or ransacked by an airport employee, it will likely be the designer bag. Buy good quality luggage in a nice color, preferably monogrammed. My luggage choice is the luggage from Lands End. Land's End stands by their products. If a zipper tab breaks off during travel, which I've had happen many times with other suitcases and only once with my LE luggage, just call and they'll send replacements--even to India.

Body Odor - Not yours, someone else's. Let's face it, everyone eventually ends up sitting next to someone on a plane they would prefer not to. Welcome to the realities of travel. I recently received a good tip from an expat friend in England (Thank You Sharee). Instead of the regular hand sanitizer that we all know and love (and use by the gallon), check out the antibacterial gels and hand lotions from Bath and Body Works. They have a lovely scent. Normally, I try not to pollute the air on an airplane with smelly products (or food), however sometimes you just need to freshen the air around you. This stuff works like a charm. Clean your hands with the gel or lotion, wave your hands around a little to dry. Fresh scents galore for a 2' radius. These babies come in 2 and 3 oz. sizes so they travel well...just make sure they're in a ziploc bag! I recently took a gnarly flight and you wouldn't believe how moisturized my hands were by the time I arrived at my destination! Repeat as necessary.

Travel wallet - The best travel wallet, in my opinion, is one that has the following features: zippered closure so nothing will fall out, a coin pocket on the outside so there is no need to for peeping eyes to see inside the wallet when counting out coins, and multiple sections inside the wallet like an accordion file for separate currencies. I just found a very nice (and affordable) Denver Hayes wallet at Mark's Work Warehouse in Canada.

Receipts - Do not throw away ATM or cash register receipts. Double check that your debit or credit card number isn't printed in full on the receipt. And while you're distracted with your receipt, don't forget to take card out of the ATM machine. Been there, done that.

Traveling With Children - Recently, we were on a flight where a child screamed blue murder from beginning to end. For the entire three and a half hours people were visibly perturbed. Traveling with children requires preparation--and stamina. Bring snacks, entertainment, and patience!

Noise - I'm talking about the screaming kids or the seat-mate who wants to talk your ear off. I'm a big fan of noise-canceling headphones. Bose brand are the best but they're also pricey. There are many more affordable options for good quality headphones. The best features to look for include rechargeable batteries, a charger that can be used in any country, and a one/two prong adapter for your in-flight movies. Pardon me? I'm sorry, I can't hear you!

Travel MP3 - I was trying to find a small product that would allow me to listen to my MP3 player in our hotel room without having to carry around a lot of additional gear and without using headphones. I looked at several types of portable docking speakers but couldn't find one that ran on a power supply other than batteries. This tip came from Connor; he suggested I take the cable that we use to connect my video iPod to the TV. Then we can play music through any TV in any country. We can watch TV or listen to music. We can charge it with a USB charger at the same time. Good tip, Connor.

Jet Lag - My answer to jet lag is Tylenol PM. No prescription is needed and I like that it doesn't leave me feeling groggy the next day. A couple of nights of good sleep makes it easier to stay awake during the day. It can turn 12 hours worth of time zones around on a dime.

Souvenirs and Collections - How do you commemorate your travels? Some people buy little statues representing the monuments they've toured. Some people buy paintings of every place they visit. I have a friend who buys a book in the language of the country she's toured. I have a collection of guide books for the places we've traveled. I also like to capture one good black and white photo to frame and hang somewhere in our house.

Traveling Light - At one time, I used to pack for every eventuality. Three outfits for one day in case the weather changed or I dropped a piece of dressing-soaked salad on myself (hey, it's happened). Now, I can travel for 3 weeks with a carry-on sized suitcase. It does mean that I have to do laundry and sometimes ironing along the way but it's worth not schlepping stuff around with me. Most decent hotels have a good laundry service and I don't mind paying for the convenience. My favorite thing to wear when I travel is a blouse. They're light and use up very little of the precious suitcase real estate. I like wraps instead of sweaters. And I never carry shampoo, soap, hair dryer, etc. I just use whatever is provided at the hotel. I'm low-maintenance that way.

Carry On - I carry a *huge* shoulder bag so I don't have to carry a purse, backpack and a camera case. In it, I always have ziploc bags, hand sanitizer, a pashmina wrap because I always get cold on the plane, MP3 player and headphones, book, mint-flavored chap stick, small travel camera, a micro umbrella, handy dandy document folder, slippers (Isotoners are good because they take up very little room and are excellent wash/wear). Add in a few snacks and a bottle of headache medicine and I'm good to go.

We're Invited

Last night, at nearly 7pm (quitting time), I received the following text message from McGyver:

> "Good evening mam, sorry 2 disturb u, u r free now, i want to meet 2 min."

I went outside and he said, "No. Inside, madame." He went to the car to get something as I went back inside the house. Then he came in with this...

He apologized repeatedly that his parents weren't here to invite us in person. He told us that is customary. There will be a bridegroom reception, the wedding ceremony and another reception in Chennai a week later.

We're honored and we're looking forward to attending his wedding celebrations.

Repatriation

No, we won't be repatriating in the foreseeable future. I dialed into a phone conference this morning on the topic of repatriation. It gave me some food for thought. It also reiterated to me how challenging repatriation is! One of the main reasons for this, as one caller commented, is that many companies hold your hand, give language and cultural training upon expatriation. However, during repatriation, there is no support. I can attest to this. The assumption is that you've come back to your home country so you know how to deal with everything. In my case, we went back to the US, but not back to the south. We moved to the mid-west. Each area of the US: New England; the Southern States; the Midwest; West Coast and Mountain States each have their own distinct "way." It's like different cultures within one country.

We moved to the US when we were young. There were some adjustments, mostly adjusting to not living near our family and some adjustments to food brands. That was actually the easiest transition of all our moves. Adjusting to England was tougher, especially adjusting to life abroad during the fallout of 9/11. I wanted to be "home" in the US. More adjusting when we repatriated back to a different state in the US. I felt

confused a lot but at the end of the day it was just another new place to settle in to and I got on with it.

During one of my rough days, Jb asked, "Is there anywhere you think you could be happy?"

It's not that I was unhappy, I was just in a constant cycle of change. It was only years later that I read some books about expatriation and repatriation. It was only then that I realized the feelings I had were normal. I wasn't a discontented, maladjusted person.

There are times when I think it's an absolute wonder that I'm as sane as I am. Especially when my next thought is--I wonder where we'll go next? Not back to the US yet, I hope.

11 Month Evaluation

We've now lived in India for 11 months. It may have been our home leave trip or the fact that we've just lived here long enough for me to march my way through each step of culture shock. Maybe it's because my husband has 'pimped by bathroom' and now I have enough hot water take a decent bath (don't underestimate the effects of a happy tub), but I'm in a good place. I feel calmer and less stressed out. Things don't aggravate me like they did around the 7-8 month mark. I'm more patient too. I've learned how to deal with having so many people around me at home and when I'm out. I'm getting better at making conscious choices about how I spend time instead of getting caught up in the current and then regretting getting sucked into things I didn't really want to do.

As I've been reading back through the stories of our first year here, I can clearly identify each of these four phases. What a journey this year has been!

1. Tourist or Honeymoon Phase

2. Emptiness or Rejection Phase

3. The Conformist Phase

4. Assimilation Phase or Complete Adjustment

-According to http://www.doctortravel.ca/tips/culture_shock/

Back in August, I posted about Culture Shock and at the time I thought I was somewhere between phases 2 and 3. I think I bounced back and forth for a period of time while dipping my toes occasionally into phase 4. My mini identity crisis had me trying to conform and rejecting my host country at the same time.

I believe I'm well-rooted in the Assimilation Phase now, although I'm sure I'll regress once in a while (when the frustrations occasionally build up). I'm much more comfortable. Now I feel like I'm getting the hang of India. The differences between my home country and host country aren't so blinding, they're blending into the background. At the end of the Repatriation Webinar that I dialed into last week, the presenter left us with something to think about. She asked, "What cultural gift or golden nugget has your host country given to you to take back to your home country?"

I don't think I have that answer yet. But what I do know is that I'm ready to receive that gift. I'm looking forward to the experiences ahead from which I'll be able to draw out my golden nugget.

Note from the author:

At the beginning of 2007, I didn't set out to write a book. I started a blog to keep my friends and family up to date with our lives in India. Little did I know that journaling about the wonders of India, and the frustrations, would turn out to be such a fantastic outlet for me. Once I typed it out and hit the "publish" button, it was like something was released.

I've been on a steep learning curve and well outside my comfort zone since we relocated to India. I faced my inner-diva, which I didn't even know I had, and came to terms with what it would take for me to settle into living in a country that made me so uncomfortable. It was never that I was unhappy, because how can a person with so much look around this place and whine about their life? It was purely culture shock. A classic textbook case of it. I hate to sound like a cliche, but it really does take time. Some expats are free to come and go on assignment, but those of us with school-age children have a greater challenge and must find a way to come to terms with living in a different culture quickly because we set the tone for the rest of the family. For me, that meant almost a year--I've always been a little slow. Depending upon the assignment and an expat's experience, this can go fairly smoothly, or it can take more time like it did for me in India. Most of the time, I feel in control, open-minded, and ready to fill my suitcase with as many images and experiences as possible.

When discussing this year's journey with an expat friend, she said, "It's like an arc." Inspiration hit me. The top of the arc is the height of an expat's discomfort and dissatisfaction. Luckily, coming back down the other side, the arc is transformed into a colorful rainbow, and we know what's at the end of a rainbow!

Thank you for joining me on the journey of my expat arc. Best wishes for a pot filled with priceless treasures and golden nuggets that await you at the end of your expat arc too.

Praise for Earth to Danie

www.earthtodanie.com

"So far, it's been great to read...so, don't stop." –Richard G.

"Have you ever thought about writing a book? You describe things so 'auspiciously." - Lisette W.

"I hope this means you are working on a book or some other great literary piece of work. You are a tremendous writer. Please keep writing!" - Janet D.

"I checked out some of your photos, I swear you could write a book and it would be a best seller!!! It is incredible what you are encountering and I admire your stride and attitude in getting through the challenges. You all have grown so much in such a way that we can't even imagine." – Pam B.

"Oh my gosh girl, you are quite a comedian when it comes to writing. You really should write a book about all of these experiences, or even, put all of your blogs in a book." - Penny B.

"I am hooked on your blog. It is the first thing I check each morning after loading up my laptop. I wish you would start to write books." – Janet D.

"I've been reading through your blog. I envy and admire you -- it sure ain't been easy! I'm looking forward to hearing about your adventures in India…" - Kim J.

"OK, I was just perusing your blog. If I had taken the time to do that before I put mine up, I probably never would have done it! Yours is so cool, mine is so dull. I humbly bow before you, the queen of blogging... !" -Lynn V.

"Hey baby! I've been keeping up with your blog. I love it. Makes me laugh." – Bonnie S.

"I have saved your Blog page to my favorites so I can check out your journey once in a while. PS: You could really be a writer!!" - Shannan J.

"LOVE THE BLOG!" - Kelly R.

"I admire your honesty about having culture shook and living in India. I believe that this blog will help others who may have to move overseas, they will have some idea of what to expect living abroad......mainly me!!!" - Asmaa C.

"Well then....you will have to just start that "book" we are all encouraging you to write! We are sure it will be a best seller." - Pam B.

"I love reading your blog..." – Kim J.

"Your blog is great....you're a wonderful writer! Your descriptions and phrases crack me up!"..."This is certainly nothing like A Passage to India. Oh my goodness"..."Your writing is certainly riveting." -Dianne H.

"Great Blog Danie!! " - Stephanie T.

"I think you should publish your blog as it is really an outstanding description of an amazing journey we have all been on for a long time." - JB

100